Internally Displaced Persons and the Law in Nigeria

I0123683

This book examines the national legal frameworks in place for internally displaced people in Nigeria and considers how they can be extended to provide further legal protection.

Despite a growing global awareness of the importance of developing solutions to the problem of internal displacement, how that translates to national level response is often under-researched. This book focuses on Nigeria, where conflict and violence continue to drive high levels of displacement. The book begins by examining the definitions and causes of internal displacement in the national context, before considering the state of national law, and the applicability of the Kampala Convention for furthering protection and assistance for internally displaced persons.

This book will be of interest to researchers of African studies and internal displacement, as well as to policy makers, civil society organisations, humanitarian actors and other regional and international stakeholders.

Aderomola Adeola is Assistant Director, Centre for Refugee Studies, York University, Canada.

Routledge Studies on Law in Africa
Series Editor: Makau W. Mutua

The Constitution and Governance in Cameroon
Laura-Stella E. Enonchong

Internally Displaced Persons and the Law in Nigeria
Aderomola Adeola

Internally Displaced Persons and the Law in Nigeria

Aderomola Adeola

R Routledge
Taylor & Francis Group

LONDON AND NEW YORK

First published 2022
by Routledge
2 Park Square, Milton Park, Abingdon, Oxon OX14 4RN

and by Routledge
605 Third Avenue, New York, NY 10158

Routledge is an imprint of the Taylor & Francis Group, an informa business

© 2022 Aderomola Adeola

The right of Aderomola Adeola to be identified as author of this work has been asserted in accordance with sections 77 and 78 of the Copyright, Designs and Patents Act 1988.

British Library Cataloguing-in-Publication Data
A catalogue record for this book is available from the British Library

Library of Congress Cataloging-in-Publication Data
Names: Adeola, Romola, 1989- author.
Title: Internally displaced persons and the law in Nigeria/Romola Adeola.
Description: New York: Routledge, 2021. | Includes bibliographical references and index.
Identifiers: LCCN 2021032595 (print) | LCCN 2021032596 (ebook) |
ISBN 9780367703837 (hardback) | ISBN 9780367703851 (paperback) |
ISBN 9781003146025 (ebook)
Subjects: LCSH: Internally displaced persons–Legal status, laws, etc.–Nigeria. |
Forced migration–Nigeria.
Classification: LCC KTA1472 .A93 2021 (print) | LCC KTA1472 (ebook) |
DDC 342.66908/3–dc23
LC record available at https://lccn.loc.gov/2021032595
LC ebook record available at https://lccn.loc.gov/2021032596

ISBN: 978-0-367-70383-7 (hbk)
ISBN: 978-0-367-70385-1 (pbk)
ISBN: 978-1-003-14602-5 (ebk)

DOI: 10.4324/9781003146025

Typeset in Times New Roman
by Deanta Global Publishing Services, Chennai, India

DEDICATION
Soli Deo (Yeshua) Gloria

Contents

1 Context

1.1 Introduction

The issue of internal displacement has emerged as a major issue in contemporary Nigerian society. Given the prevalence of the challenge in many parts of the country, the need to provide a significant solution to the issue has emerged. This resonates both in relation to the magnitude of those displaced and the plethora of issues that account for internal displacement in the country. While internal displacement in post-colonial Nigeria is a challenge that dates to the early periods of independence, notably the Biafran civil war from 1967–1970,[1] contemporary Nigeria has significantly experienced a wave of growing internal displacement concerns, from the insurgent activities of the Boko Haram group to the onset of natural disasters including climate change. While there is a prevalent consensus that addressing the issue of internal displacement is imperative, knowing who these persons are is fundamental to curating solutions. This is because the protection dimension of these persons is not covered by refugee law. Rather, internally displaced persons (IDPs) remain within the borders of the state of displacement and as such protection is primarily with states in which they are displaced.

Over the last two decades, a plethora of research has flourished on the importance of legal protection for IDPs in various parts of the world. Precipitated on the wheels of global protection through the UN Guiding Principles on Internal Displacement (Guiding Principles),[2] there is now a consensus that these persons are a category of forced migrants for which protection and assistance are essential.[3] Within several national contexts, understanding the nature of existing legal protection has become imperative as a step towards fostering sustainable solutions. This is also an imperative in the Nigerian context given the prevalence of the issue and the pertinence of finding durable solutions to the issue of internal displacement. It is within this context that this book finds expression, considering the law on internal displacement in Nigeria.

DOI: 10.4324/9781003146025-1

1.2 Migrants, refugees and internally displaced persons: clarification

Integral to the history of societies is migration and human mobilities. And this narrative evidently resonates in the way in which societies across Africa have been formed. Embedded in the histories of the plurality of cultures across Nigeria is the diversity of movement from within and outside the continent.

Pre-colonially for instance, the narrative of mobilities was conditioned upon 'trade, trade routes, markets, religions, diplomacy, wars, conquests and slave trade'.[4] For instance, the founding figure of the Borgu royal lineages – which spanned parts of the north-west region of Nigeria and the northern parts of Benin – was said to have originally migrated from Persia (pre-Islamic Iran).[5] This founding figure (Kisra) derived his name from 'the term Kisrā, which is used in classical Arabic sources as the title of the Sasanian rulers of pre-Islamic Iran.'[6] A cursory look at the histories of other notable empires and kingdoms including the Ibibio Kingdom, the Kanem-Bornu empire, the Nri Kingdom, the Oyo empire and the Kwararafa Kingdom reflect the centrality of mobilities to the socio-cultural formation and emergence of the Nigerian state.[7]

Movements during the colonial epoch were mostly linked to colonial capital given the emergence of export-oriented plantations. As such, in this period, labour migration was a prevalent feature. Aworawo observes, for instance, that from 'the mid-1930s, Nigerians came to dominate the labor that sustained Equatorial Guinea's cocoa and coffee plantation'.[8] Sundiata observes that by the year 1941 'there were 10,000 Nigerians already on Bioko. This number increased throughout the decade. In 1954–1955 a very conservative estimate of the total number of Nigerian migrants on the island was "about 15,800"'.[9] However, by the mid-1960s, Nigerians comprised about 85,000 of 100,000 people on the island, 'two-thirds of these Nigerians were Igbo-, Ibibio-, and Efik-speaking'.[10] At least three factors drove this narrative. According to Sundiata 'recruiters were generously paid by Spanish officials and employers. Second, there was pressure to pay taxes to the British colonial administration in Nigeria. And third, there was demographic pressure'.[11] But this was not solely the reality in Nigeria. Across various parts of the continent, there were seasonal movements to farms, mines and plantations with and across borders, that were sometimes strictly induced by the colonial administration.

With the attainment of political independence and the emergence of colonial nation-states, the narrative on movements began to shift towards the consolidation of national identities as constructed in national immigration policies and programs. With the retention of the Berlin borders, the post-colonial state redefined patterns of movement along the lines of national belonging. And this significantly shaped the socio-economic narrative, in some instances resulting in toxic exclusions and the negative labelling of those who did not belong to the legally constructed notion of citizenship and nationality. According to Peil, the 'achievement of independence, provided several countries with an opportunity to get rid of "strangers" in their midst'.[12] For instance, Peil observes that 'Ghana deported some Nigerians in 1954, and some Voltaics [Burkinabés] in 1961, because "their presence was not conducive to the public good"'.[13] The undulations in national economic development were also in certain instances, conflated with the presence of non-nationals. And this resulted in cases of mass expulsions, for instance, of non-nationals including Ghanaians from Nigerians in the 1980s.[14] According to Aluko,[15]

> The parlous state of the economy had also contributed to the expulsion order. As a result of the combination of mismanagement, inefficiency, and unparalleled official corruption, and the glut in oil world market, the economy that was relatively buoyant throughout most of the seventies slumped by early 1981. Instead of the real growth rate of 7.2 per cent envisaged under the Four Year Development Plan 1981–5 there was only a growth rate of 2 per cent in 1981, and this fell below 1 per cent in 1982. The balance of payments surplus of the country that stood at ₦2,402.6 billion in 1980 turned to a deficit of ₦1,500 million in 1982. The foreign reserves of the country that amounted to ₦5,648.2 million in December 1980 had fallen to about ₦780 million at the end of 1982. The public debt that stood at ₦9,922.3 million in 1980 had risen to ₦12 billion at the end of 1982.
>
> The austerity measures that were introduced in April 1982 had done little to improve the economy. Inflation in 1982 reached a record level of over 25 per cent. Unemployment (including graduate unemployment) had reached an alarming proportion of nearly 20 per cent of the work force. And more unemployment was daily being created by manufacturing and construction companies who could not easily import raw materials and spare parts, because of the austerity measures of the Shagari government. Given all these factors, then, expelling the illegal aliens must have been tempting if partly as a scape-goat measure for the failures of the government and partly as a popular move to create jobs for thousands of Nigerians in an election year. Alhaji Ali Baba said on 25 January 1983 that one of the reasons for the expulsion order was to create job opportunities for Nigerians.

The post-colonial preservation of the in-group and out-group narratives on identities with evident colonial links shaped the laws and policies of newly independent states from the early periods of independence. Over the last decades, national governance of migration and mobilities has been orchestrated through prisms of national security and in some instances, criminal justice.[16] However, these approaches are mostly a consequence of negative binaries and systemic crisis of reception and mobilities management.

The existence of uneven patterns of laws and practices on migration and mobilities across the continent has led to an increasing call for effective governance at various levels that addresses the causes of movement (specifically in contexts where these are negative), protect various categories of persons (along the spectrum of voluntary to forcibly moved populations) and reinforce the continental drive towards unification. In developing solutions, it is useful to underscore the fact that the causes for migration and mobilities are not monolithic and this suggests an inherent complexity.

The patterns of migration and mobilities evidently reinforce the fact that there are several reasons why people move. While many of the movements in pre-colonial times were directed towards seizing on new opportunities, there were movements brought about by inter-tribal conflicts such as in the conquest of lands and territories. Moreover, there was the trans-Atlantic slave trade in which an estimated '12.5 million people were forced out of Africa'.[17] As earlier observed, during the colonial era, labour-oriented mobilities were a significant feature. Though there were also forced movements due to inter-tribal wars, uprisings against colonial administrations and clashes. In post-colonial Africa, voluntary and involuntary dimensions of mobilities have also emerged linked to a plethora of factors including labour, conflict, socio-economic opportunities, education, and in more recent years, disasters linked to climate change. In the Revised Migration Policy Framework for Africa and Plan of Action (Revised Migration Policy Framework for Africa), it is observed that[18]

> The root causes of migration in Africa are numerous and inter-related. The push-pull framework provides insight into this complex web of factors. Lack of socio-economic opportunities and the rule of law, poor governance, patronage and corruption, political instability, conflict, terrorism and civil strife are major push factors. Pull factors include the real or perceived opportunities for a better life, higher income, improved security, and superior education and health care in countries of destination. The push-pull dynamic is intensified by a number of other factors that facilitate migration. These include the lower costs of migration; improved communication, especially social media and the internet; greater information availability; and the need to join relatives, families and friends. The movement of people – voluntary or forced,

legal or undocumented, within or across borders – is a complex process that affects policy making in a wide range of areas.

And along the verse spectrum of causes of migration and mobilities, normative frameworks have also defined categories and structured governance. In this context, the use of the word 'migration' or the term 'migrants' is often employed with respect to populations moving voluntarily. While such movements may be internal, much of the emphasis of migration governance from global and regional perspectives relates to the international dimension of these forms of movement. Within this context, movements may be regular or irregular. The spectrum of regular movements is often defined with reference to immigration laws and policies. Within this context are a broad group, based on national normative systems, which may include migrant workers, students, permanent or temporary residents and other categories of persons whose presence in a country are through the regular pathways provided within normative frameworks at national, bilateral or multilateral levels. In situations where movement patterns are not legally conditioned, they are often described as irregular migration. Essentially, these are movement patterns that 'take place outside the laws, regulations, or international agreements governing the entry into or exit from the State of origin, transit or destination'.[19] While there are several frameworks that reflect pertinent aspects of migration, international migration governance is incorporated, at the global level, in the Global Compact on Safe, Orderly and Regular Migration (GCM).[20] As a 'milestone in the history of the global dialogue and international cooperation on migration',[21] the GCM 'offers a 360-vision of international migration'.[22] Underlying its formation are key principles, including its people-centred focus, sustainable development, human rights, rule of law, gender-responsiveness and a whole-of-society approach. While incorporating the principle of national sovereignty and recognising that '[s]tates may distinguish between regular and irregular migration status',[23] the GCM emphasises the commitment of states to[24]

> adapt options and pathways for regular migration in a manner that facilitates labour mobility and decent work reflecting demographic and labour market realities, optimizes education opportunities, upholds the right to family life, and responds to the needs of migrants in a situation of vulnerability, with a view to expanding and diversifying availability of pathways for safe, orderly and regular migration.

At the regional level, the Revised Migration Policy Framework for Africa provides a ten-year strategic plan across thematic areas, formulating guidance to various actors at different levels to enhance migration governance.

At the national level, the main legislation regulating international migration in Nigeria is the Immigration Act.[25] In 2015, a National Migration Policy was adopted which establishes a governance framework on migration and presents a more contemporary narrative with a reflection on rights-based governance strategies, gender dimensions and themes such as climate change. However, the policy framework tends to define migration broadly to include forced migration. In this sense, it does not adopt a clear-cut bifurcation but rather takes a generic approach to the discourse. For instance, it defines migration as a 'geographic movement of people across a specified boundary for the purpose of establishing a new permanent or semi-permanent residence'.[26] No distinction is drawn based on voluntariness. The National Migration Policy further locates internal displacement in the context of internal migration, emphasising the fact that internal displacement 'is an important aspect of *internal migration* which occurs when people are forced or compelled to leave their homes due to environmental factors, conflict, wars, ethnic strife or natural disasters'.[27] Evidently, there are times when internal migration may conflate with internal displacement. The fact that both categories of persons remain within state borders, move from their places of residence and may leverage mobility as a coping strategy create similarities. Their movements may also be long-term or circular. However, it is pertinent to emphasise that the notion of 'forced' movement makes it imperative to pay particular attention to IDPs as a distinct category as vulnerabilities may be exacerbated. Cantor and Apollo observe, for instance, that the[28]

> reduced access [of IDPs] to social and capital assets left behind, such as housing and land, sets them apart from many other internal migrants. IDPs also seem to experience significantly worse poverty and labour market outcomes than most other internal migrants, an effect which appears long-lasting (and gendered), and are more likely to suffer conflict-related trauma. Indeed, where the situation of IDPs is not quickly stabilised, they seem to enter a vicious circle of impoverishment and marginality, and can end up over-represented among the poor and extreme poor of their countries. Thus, for both individuals and societies, internal displacement can produce a distinctive impact.

In the National Migration Policy, the element of volition is also reinforced as a defining character of IDP movement. The policy emphasises that IDPs 'are usually compelled to move from their regular place of abode while other internal migrants move of their own volition, usually for employment, family reunification or other reasons'.[29]

In the context of forced migration, it is crucial to delineate IDPs as a distinct category from refugees. While the next chapter will examine IDPs in more detail, it is useful to provide a conceptual clarity on IDPs vis-à-vis refugees. The corpus of contemporary refugee law dates back to the Second World War with the humanitarian situation in Europe as a consequence of the war. In response to the situation of persons in need of protection outside their countries of origin, the global refugee regime emerged: with the 1951 UN Refugee Convention and subsequently with a 1967 Protocol in response to the geographic limitation and dateline of the 1951 Convention.[30] But prior to the 1967 Protocol, the Organisation of African Unity (OAU) began preparing a draft regional convention. This was later adopted as a regional complement to the 1951 Convention which became generally applicable.[31]

While there are specific similarities between IDPs and refugees in terms of movement from initial points of displacement and applicability of human rights and humanitarian law in certain contexts, a fundamental difference relates to the destination of movement. Plainly, IDPs remain within state borders. But refugees move across state borders. As refugee protection functions on the basis of alienage, protection rests with the state of asylum. This is incorporated in the textual definitions in refugee law instruments, principally through the phrase of being 'outside' one's country of origin or nationality. For stateless persons, refugee protection derives from being 'outside' the country of 'habitual residence'. In the global framework, refugees are persons outside their countries of origin or habitual residence 'owing to a well-founded fear of being persecuted for reasons of race, religion, nationality, membership of a particular social group or political opinion'.[32]

The OAU 1969 Refugee Convention expands on the definition of refugees, providing that refugees are persons compelled to leave their countries of origin or habitual residence due to 'external aggression, occupation, foreign domination or events seriously disturbing public order in either part or the whole of his country of origin or nationality'.[33] IDPs, on the other hand, remain within the state of displacement and reasons for flight are more expansive within the descriptions provided in global and regional texts. In the Nigerian context, this definition is further reflected in the National Commission for Refugees (Establishment, Etc.) Act. In the third Schedule of the Act which incorporates the OAU Refugee Convention, the term 'refugee' refers to[34]

1. [...] every person who, owing to well-founded fear of being persecuted for reasons of race, religion, nationality, membership of a particular social group or political opinion, is outside the country of his nationality and is unable or, owing to such fear, is unwilling to avail himself

of the protection of that country, or who, not having a nationality and being outside the country of his former habitual residence as a result of such events, is unable or, owing to such fear, unwilling to return to it.

2. [...] also apply to every person who, owing to external aggression, occupation, foreign domination or events seriously disturbing public order in either part or the whole of his country of origin or nationality, is compelled to leave his place of habitual residence in order to seek refuge in another place outside his country of origin or nationality.

Within the Nigerian context, this book is concerned with IDPs and not refugees. For the purpose of this book, the description of the Guiding Principles and the Kampala Convention is utilised in the discussion of IDPs. For clarity, IDPs are[35]

persons or groups of persons who have been forced or obliged to flee or to leave their homes or places of habitual residence, in particular as a result of or in order to avoid the effects of armed conflict, situations of generalized violence, violations of human rights or natural or human-made disasters, and who have not crossed an internationally recognized state border.

1.3 The essence of law

There is a question as to the pertinence of the law in the furtherance of understanding issues. There are four imperatives. First is the imperative of the law as the foundation of societal order. The law as such is the propeller of actions and the basis on which society oscillates. The law as societal foundation ensures that there is clarity on the nature of the social contract on which the society is formed. Moreover, it weighs and legitimises processes and seeks to restrict the arbitrary exercise of will outside of an agreed societal prescription.

Second, there is the importance of the law, specifically as a pertinent optic for advancing sustainable solutions to societal issues. The fact that the law operates on the basis of constituted authority and derives validation from this process, makes it imperative in fostering sustainable solutions. The law provides prescriptions, one for which actors at various levels of governance may be held to account. In this sense, there is an impetus of law as integral to the process of resolving challenges. Without doubt, there is a global consensus on this importance in view of a plethora of responses to daunting challenges.

Third, understanding the law is also imperative in understanding the state of consensus on an issue and areas where improvements are required in strengthening the societal response. On the issue of internal displacement, knowing what the law prescribes is crucial in developing guidance at various levels of governance. This is crucial both for the purpose of introspection by states and extrospection by a plethora of other actors in the furtherance of protection and assistance to IDPs. It is pertinent to reflect on what the law is in this context also to address differences in legal knowledge formations at various levels of governance. This understanding is relevant in driving normative coherence on the core narratives on what protection and assistance fundamentally entail.

Fourth, there is also the significance of the law as a reinforcement of commitments and will, one which may be constantly demanded from state mechanisms and activist forces outside these mechanisms. This is important in view of the consistent rhetoric on political will and the pertinence of driving this will towards solutions to various issues. In the context of internal displacement, the law offers a basis on which to precipitate such political will in view of the fact that it operates on the paradigm of obligations from which compliance is generally required from states. And where norms are regarded as soft law, they create a basis on which to reinforce such commitments given that they offer texts on which to dialogue with states on existing concerns.

1.4 Sources of Nigerian law

It is useful to consider the sources of Nigerian law to understand the legal context of the discussion on IDP protection in the country. From the start, it is essential to emphasise that Nigeria's legal system is comprised of primary and secondary sources.[36] These sources are considered in turn.

1.4.1 Primary sources

The primary sources are the Constitution, legislations, the received English law, case laws or judicial precedent and customary law.

1.4.1.1 Constitution

As the primary source of law, the Constitution is supreme and this is reinforced in its provision that if any law is 'inconsistent' with its provisions, such 'law shall, to the extent of its inconsistency, be void'.[37] The Constitution includes a bill of rights in Chapter IV, mostly comprising of civil and political rights, and has a set of directive principles of state policy in Chapter II. The Constitution, among others, sets out the composition of national governance. It establishes various arms of governance: executive, legislative and judiciary.

Besides establishing the governance arms, the Constitution also provides for three tiers of governance: federal (or national), state (or sub-national) and local. In dividing powers across these three tiers of governance, the Constitution lists specific items around which the competences of these tiers are established. Specifically, between the federal (or national), state (or sub-national) governments, the Second Schedule to the Constitution sets out legislative competences.[38] Matters relating to the exclusive legislative list fall within the exclusive competence of the federal (or national) legislature – the National Assembly.[39] There is also a concurrent legislative list which spells out matters that fall within the competence of both the federal (National Assembly) and state (House of Assembly).[40]

However, matters that are neither contained in these lists are called 'residual' matters. In the case of the *Attorney-General of the Federation v Attorney-General of Lagos State*, the Supreme Court of Nigeria emphasised that 'Residual Matters which are matters not in either Exclusive or Concurrent Lists are matters within the exclusive competence of the State to legislate upon'.[41] In such matters, the state (House of Assembly) has exclusive competence.[42]

However, there have been instances where the National Assembly (at the federal level) had legislated on a residual matter.[43] Such was the case with the adoption of the Child's Rights Act of 2003 (CRA) which domesticates the Convention on the Rights of the Child (CRC) and the African Charter on the Rights and Welfare of the Child (ACRWC).[44] However, this law is only binding on the Federal Capital Territory (FCT) Abuja which is not one of the 36 states of the federation but rather the administrative headquarter of the country. In giving expression to the law at the state level, states laws have had to be adopted. However, there are some states that are yet to adopt legislation in this regard.

It is imperative to emphasise these competences in view of the discussion in this book. This is because the issue of internal displacement is one of such 'residual' matters as it is neither contained in the exclusive list for the federal legislative arm nor is it explicitly provided within the concurrent list. As earlier stated, the Constitution allows the National Assembly to make laws to give effect to an international treaty that is not contained in the federal exclusive legislative list.[45] However, section 12(3) of the Constitution provides that such

> bill for an Act of the National Assembly passed pursuant to the provisions of subsection (2) [for the implementation of a treaty relating to a matter not contained in the exclusive legislative list] ... shall not be enacted unless it is ratified by a majority of all the Houses of Assembly in the Federation.[46]

This provision is particularly significant for the implementation of a treaty on internal displacement, for instance, the Kampala Convention. Drawing on lessons from the CRA, it is imperative to have concurrence, particularly from the state (or sub-national) governments in order to avoid implementation challenges.[47]

1.4.1.2 Legislations

Legislations are a significant source of Nigerian law. Next to the Constitution which is the fundamental law, legislations are the norms that make up the majority of the Nigerian legal corpus. These legislations include statutes and subsidiary or delegated legislations. The corpus of the statute law may be sub-divided into five forms: Acts, Laws, Decrees, Edicts and Ordinances.

Acts are used to refer to legislations at the federal level, passed by the National Assembly. Laws are used to refer to legislations adopted at state level, passed by the House of Assembly. Given the many years of military presence on the scene of national governance in Nigeria, Decrees (at the federal military level) and Edicts (at state levels) have also been part of the Nigerian legal system. For instance, the Land Use Decree (1979) and the African Charter on Human and Peoples' Rights (Ratification and Enforcement) Decree of 1983. Another source of statutes are ordinances which were in force by 1 October 1954. Ordinances were introduced by section 57 of the Nigerian (Constitution) Order in Council of 1954 which made ordinances in force on 1 October 1954 part of Nigeria's law.[48] Over the years, however, those ordinances (which have not been repealed) have been modified and are mostly reflected as Acts within the legislative context.

While there is no specific legisliation on internal displacement, there are several normative frameworks that relate to the issue of protection and assistance to IDPs. Evidently, these are norms relating to human rights, humanitarian law and environmental law among others. These norms may be utilised in certain instances that relate to IDP protection within these contexts.

Aside from statutes, there are also subsidiary legislations developed by persons, bodies and institutions enabled by law. In *Njoku & Ors v Iheanatu & Ors*, the Court of Appeal, per Garba JCA, explained that a subsidiary legislation is 'one that was subsequently made or enacted under and pursuant to the power conferred by the principal legislation or enactment. It derives its force and efficacy from the principal legislation to which it is therefore secondary and complimentary.'[49] These legislations may take several forms, such as 'any order, rules, regulations, rules of court or bye-laws'.[50] Subsidiary legislations have the 'the force of law'.[51] A relevant example of a subsidiary legislation is the Fundamental Rights (Enforcement Procedure)

Rules of 2009 (FREPR) developed by the former Chief Justice of Nigeria based on section 46(3) of the Constitution.[52] The FREPR provides that[53]

> [a]ny person who alleges that any of the Fundamental Rights provided for in the Constitution or African Charter on Human and Peoples' Rights (Ratification and Enforcement) Act and to which he is entitled, has been, is being, or is likely to be infringed, may apply to the Court in the State where the infringement occurs or is likely to occur, for redress.

The relevance of this provision is that it allows human rights litigation based on the violation of the African Charter on Human and Peoples' Rights,[54] which is significant given the fact that this is a regional instrument, domesticated by the state. In *Master v Mansur & Ors*, the Court of Appeal, per Abiru JCA, observed that[55]

> The human rights law of Nigeria is contained, *inter alia*, in two major documents. These are the 1999 Constitution of the Federal Republic of Nigeria and the African Charter on Human and Peoples' Rights, domesticated as the African Charter on Human and Peoples' Rights (Ratification and Enforcement) Act, Cap 10 Laws of the Federation of Nigeria 1990.

1.4.1.3 Received English Law

English law is one of the primary sources of Nigerian law given the political history of the country under British rule and the introduction of the English legal system in the country during this period. It is from this body of law that the legal regime significantly resonates. As with most of the Commonwealth, the impact of the English law on the legal landscape cannot be underemphasised. Evidently, it is from this system that the structure of legislations has also been erected. Howbeit with some differences that cohere with the contemporary legal landscape in the country and the region. Moreover, the independence of the country on 1 October 1960 as with post-colonial developments, over the last six decades, has resulted in a significant legal shift from a sole incorporation of English law to other domestic forms of law-making. However, the influence of English law remains a compelling legacy, both in law and practice.

There are two forms of English law in the Nigerian legal system. There is the English law that extends to Nigeria, made before 1 October 1960. These are laws that are applicable unless repealed by a specific Nigerian legislation.[56] On the other hand, there is the Received English Law which mainly comprises: (a) the English common law, (b) doctrines of equity, (c) the statute of general application which was in force in England on 1 January 1900, and (d) statutes and subsidiary legislation on specific matters. Section 32(1) of the Interpretation Act recognises these laws, providing that[57]

> Subject to the provisions of this section and except in so far as other provision is made by any Federal law, the common law of England and the doctrines of equity, together with the statutes of general application that were in force in England on the 1st day of January, 1900, shall, in so far as they relate to any matter within the legislative competence of the Federal legislature, be in force in Nigeria.

However, on the extent of the application of English law, the Supreme Court in *Kalu v Odili & Ors*, per Nnaemeka-Agu JSC, emphasised that[58]

> Where there is a local legislation on a point at issue, then that should be interpreted and applied to the situation; no matter what English Courts decided on the point. Where, however, the English decision is based on an English statute which is in pari materia with our local enactment or on a principle of the common law or equity which has been received in Nigeria, then such a decision will usually be followed by the Nigerian Court. Conversely, when there is local legislation on an issue, the Nigerian Court has no business with an English statute, excepting, of course. It is in pari materia with the Nigerian statute, so that decisions of competent English Courts on such in pari materia statutes will have persuasive effect on the Nigerian Court.

1.4.1.4 Case laws/judicial precedents

Embedded in the hierarchy of courts within the Nigerian legal system, judicial precedents resonate from the fact that decisions of the higher courts are binding on lower courts. In *Sheka v Bashari*, the Court of Appeal, per Abiru JCA, emphasised that the[59]

> doctrine of judicial precedent postulates that where the facts in a subsequent case are similar or close as facts in an earlier case that had been decided upon, judicial pronouncements in the earlier case are subsequently utilized to govern and determine the decision in the subsequent case – *Nwangwu Vs Ukachukwu* (2000) 6 NWLR (Pt 662) 674. The doctrine recognizes that decisions of Court draw their inspiration and strength from the facts which framed the issues for decision and once such decisions are made they control future judgment in like

or similar cases, hence the facts of two cases must either be the same or at least similar before a decision in the earlier case can be used in a later case.

In *Nigeria Arab Bank Ltd v Barri Engineering Nig Ltd* (*Barri* case), the Supreme Court, per Ogundare JSC, made the point that the doctrine '(otherwise called stare decisis) requires all subordinate courts to follow decisions of superior courts'.[60] However, not every judicial pronouncement is binding.[61] What is binding is the reason for the decision, the principle of law upon which the case is based or put differently, the *ratio decidendi*.

Evidently, obiter dictum, or statements made in passing will not constitute precedence. Rather, precedent is established on 'the legal reasoning that led to the court's decision'.[62] The challenge, however, is where this is made wrongly. However, in the *Barri* case, the Supreme Court, per Ogundare JSC, reinforced the fact that such decisions are binding 'even where these decisions are obviously wrong having been based upon a false premise; this is the "foundation on which the consistency of our judicial decision is based"'.[63] In horizontal relationships, however, as between courts of coordinate jurisdictions, precedents are persuasive.

1.4.1.5 Customary law

Customary laws are local laws, mostly within two main categories: ethnic and Sharia laws. While the latter derives from the Islamic religion, the former derives from the ethnic plurality across the Nigerian state. Given the heterogeneous nature of the country, there are several customary laws in existence. Much of these laws are unwritten, passed through generations. The flexibility and adaptability of customary law makes it a dynamic legal corpus.[64] In *Oyewunmi & Anor v Ogunesan*, the Supreme Court, per Obaseki JSC, emphasised that customary law (ethnic law) is[65]

> organic or living law of the indigenous people of Nigeria regulating their lives and transactions. It is organic in that it is not static. It is regulatory in that it controls the lives and transactions of the community subject to it. It is said that custom is a mirror of the culture of the people.

A question of facts,[66] customary (ethnic law) reflects the 'accepted usage and culture of a given people'.[67] However, it is subject to the repugnancy test, introduced during the colonial administration and post-colonially preserved.[68] Under this test, the court will not uphold a custom which is repugnant to natural justice, equity and good conscience. In *Ojukwu v Agupusi &*

Anor, the Court of Appeal, per Agube JCA, reiterated a prior position of the Supreme Court that[69]

> [i]n deciding whether a custom is repugnant to natural justice, equity and good conscience or contrary to public morality or policy, involves the value judgement of the Judge/Court which should be objectively relate to contemporary mores, aspirations, expectations and sensitivities of the people of this country and the consensus opinion of civilized international community which we share.

1.4.2 Secondary sources

Besides primary sources, there are pertinent secondary sources of Nigerian law that strengthen the legal corpus for the furtherance of law and practice. These secondary sources include foreign court decisions, jurist opinions/academic texts and treaties. These are considered in turn.

1.4.2.1 Foreign court decisions

Decisions of foreign courts are generally non-binding. This was reinforced by the Supreme Court in *Dada v The State*.[70] However, they have a persuasive force before domestic courts.[71] In *Agbaje v Fashola*, the Court of Appeal, per Adamu JCA, emphasised that '[f]oreign cases are merely persuasive in Nigerian courts and only become relevant when there are no relevant precedents of Nigerian courts'.[72] There have been instances where domestic courts have cited case laws from jurisdictions such as the United States, India and the United Kingdom. However, often with the point that these decisions are merely persuasive.[73]

1.4.2.2 Jurist opinions/academic texts

The writings of jurists have also been significant in the exposition of Nigerian law. Before domestic courts, for instance, these writings have been used to buttress relevant positions of the law. For instance, in *Adedeji & Sons Motors Nigeria Limited v Immeh & Anor*, the Court of Appeal made reference to the book *Practice and Procedures of the Supreme Court, Court of Appeal and High Courts in Nigeria* (1980) by Akinola Aguda. This was referenced in buttressing the point that the 'law is trite that items of claim constituting special damages have to be particularised in the plaintiff's pleading'.[74] Also, in *Attorney General of the Federation v Attorney General of Lagos State*, the Supreme Court, per Mukhtar JSC, referred to the exposition on federalism by Ben Nwabueze in the book titled *Federalism in Nigeria under the Presidential Constitution* (1983).[75]

1.4.2.3 Treaties

Treaties are also imperative sources of Nigerian law. As a member of the international community and having ratified legal texts at various governance levels including the United Nations (UN), the African Union (AU) and the Economic Community of West African States (ECOWAS), there are existing international obligations that require compliance and implementation. Under international law, a country's obligations to comply with treaty provisions are evidently upon ratification. But even upon signing treaties, a country has an obligation to ensure that it refrains from actions that will impede on the object and purpose of the treaty as emphasised under the Vienna Convention on the Law of Treaties (VCLT).[76]

However, Nigeria follows the dualist tradition by which treaties are applicable within national contexts upon domestication.[77] But this does not obviate the country of responsibility in light of the principle of *pacta sunt servanda*.[78] However, an interesting question relates to customary international law or jus cogens norms and whether these norms are only applicable upon domestication of treaties that codify them. Evidently, under international law, states cannot derogate from *jus cogen* norms and are duty bound to comply with customary international law. And such practice needs to be followed within the national context. This position is evidently unclear within the national context as the courts are yet to provide explicit clarity. However, there is an emerging weight of evidence in the scholarship to the effect that the international legal position is the preferred conclusion.[79] Evidently, the Nigerian state has also positioned itself as adherent to *jus cogen* norms such as with the prohibition of genocide, and has also demonstrated support for customary international law such as the four Geneva Conventions.

1.4.2.4 Policies

Policy frameworks are generally non-binding statements on specific issues used as a pertinent blueprint for defining the course of actions of specific institutions within the state. Traditionally, policies are not considered law as they are not made through the conventional legal-making process required for a particular instrument to be regarded as a source of law. However, they have become increasingly relevant in the normative landscape across various contexts, and they often serve as an elaborative reflection on pertinent positions of the state echoing global and regional commitments and seeking to provide a strategy for action in advancing specific objectives.

Through policies, the government has often clearly defined the position on pressing national issues. For instance, through the Nigerian Migration Policy 2015, the Nigerian government affirmed 'commitment to all existing international and national instruments, principles and standards related to migrants' and set out specific objectives it seeks to accomplish including providing 'a platform for the uniform administration of migration in Nigeria'.[80] Section 17(2) of the Nigerian Constitution recognises the capacity of the state to make policies, emphasising that[81]

The state shall direct its policy towards ensuring: (a) the promotion of a planned and balanced economic development; (b) that the material resources of the nation are harnessed and distributed as best as possible to serve the common good; (c) that the economic system is not operated in such a manner as to permit the concentration of wealth or the means of production and exchange in the hands of few individuals or of a group; and (d) that suitable and adequate shelter, suitable and adequate food, reasonable national minimum living wage, old age care and pensions, and unemployment, sick benefits and welfare of the disabled are provided for all citizens.

It is in this context that the specific framework with respect to internal displacement has been clearly defined. While a legislation is yet to emerge, the Federal Executive Council[82] adopted a policy framework on internal displacement in 2021,[83] establishing the national blueprint for protecting and assisting IDPs in Nigeria.

1.5 Scope and objective

Much of the research on forced migration has been in relation to the protection of refugees, evidently in view of the global governance of refugees and the existence of rich laws and policies at various contexts – national and regional – in the furtherance of international protection of refugees. However, not much research has emerged on the issue of internal displacement. Even while more people are being displaced within state borders than externally, research on internal displacement has been limited in comparative terms to refugees.

Early research in this field was led by the Brookings Institution through research and policies led by Francis Deng and Roberta Cohen.[84] With the end of the Brookings IDP project, it has become imperative to revive the research gap at various governance levels. It is within this context that this book finds its evident place specifically within the context of Nigeria, considering the normative protection for IDPs relevant to the national conversation on protection, regional dialogue on strengthening laws and policies and the global discussion on providing sustainable solutions to the issue of internal displacement.

The research in this book is sub-divided into four parts. The first part, which is the introductory part of this book, presents a brief context to the discussion in the book, providing clarity on similar concepts and reflecting on the Nigerian legal system. The second part of this book examines in more depth the issue of internal displacement in Nigeria, specifically reflecting on the definition and causes of internal displacement in Nigeria. The third part of this book discusses general legal frameworks for the protection of IDPs in Nigeria, reflecting on the Constitution and other relevant normative standards relating to human rights, armed conflict, migration, the environment, refugees, disaster management and land law. The fourth part examines the national policy framework on internal displacement, reflecting on the provisions of the instrument with respect to protection and assistance of IDPs. The fifth part concludes this book, reflecting on the discussion and recommendations in the furtherance of the law on internal displacement in Nigeria.

Notes

1 See Alfred O Uzokwe *Surviving in Biafra: the story of the Nigerian civil war: over two million died* (iUniverse, 2003); Frederick Forsyth *The Biafra story: the making of an African legend* (Pen & Sword Books Ltd, 2015).
2 UN Commission on Human Rights, Addendum, 'Guiding Principles on Internal Displacement' *Report of the Representative of the Secretary-General, Mr. Francis M. Deng, submitted pursuant to Commission on Human Rights resolution 1997/39*, UN Doc. E/CN.4/1998/53/Add.2 (11 February 1998); See generally UN Commission on Human Rights, *Comprehensive study on the human rights issues related to internally displaced persons*, prepared by Mr. Francis M. Deng, Representative of the Secretary-General, UN Doc E/CN.4/1993/35 (21 January 1993); UN Commission on Human Rights 'Internally displaced persons: compilation and analysis of legal norms' *Report of the Representative of the Secretary-General, Mr. Francis M Deng, submitted pursuant to the UN Commission on Human Rights resolution 1995/57*, UN Doc. E/CN.4/1996/52/ Add.2 (5 December 1995); African Union Convention for the Protection and Assistance of Internally Displaced Persons in Africa (23 October 2009) (Kampala Convention).
3 David A Korn *Exodus within borders: an introduction to the crisis of internal displacement* (Brookings Institution Press, 1999); Janie Hampton *Internally displaced people: a global survey* (Earthscan, 2002); Catherine Phuong *The international protection of internally displaced persons* (Cambridge University Press, 2004) 53–56; Francis Deng 'International response to internal displacement: a revolution in the making' (2004) 11(3) *Human Rights Brief* 1; Simon Bagshaw *Developing a normative framework for the protection of internally displaced persons* (Transactional Publishers, 2005); Thomas G Weiss and David A

Korn *Internal displacement: conceptualization and its consequences* (Routledge, 2006); Elizabeth Ferris 'Assessing the impact of the Principles: an unfinished task' (2008) *Forced Migration Review* 10; Robert K Goldman 'Internal displacement, the Guiding Principles on Internal Displacement, the principles normative status, and the need for their effective domestic implementation in Colombia' (2009) 2 *Anuario Colombiano de Derecho Internacional* 59; Phil Orchid 'Protection of internally displaced persons: soft law as a norm generating mechanism' (2010) 36(2) *Review of International Studies* 281–303; Elizabeth Ferris, Erin Mooney and Chareen Stark 'From responsibility to response: assessing national approaches to internal displacement' (The Brookings Institution – London School of Economics Project on Internal Displacement, 2011); David J Cantor *Returns of internally displaced persons during armed conflict: international law and its application in Colombia* (Brill-Nijhoff, 2018); Gabriel Cardona-Fox *Exile within borders: a global look at commitment to the international regime to protect internally displaced persons* (Brill, 2019); Romola Adeola *The internally displaced person in international law* (Edward Elgar, 2020).

4 Olayinka Akanle *Kinship networks and international migration in Nigeria* (Cambridge Scholars, 2013) 9.
5 Paolo F de Moraes Farais 'A letter from Ki-Toro Mahamman Gaani, King of Busa (Borgu, Northern Nigeria) about the "Kisra" stories of origin (c. 1910)' (1992) *Sudanic Africa* 109, 113.
6 As above.
7 Sabine Dinslage and Rudolf Leger 'Language and migration the impact of the Jukun on Chadic speaking groups in the Benue-Gongola basin' (1996) *Berichte des Sonderforschungsbereichs* 67–75.
8 David Aworawo 'Decisive thaw: the changing pattern of relations between Nigeria and Equatorial Guinea, 1980–2005' (2010) *Journal of International and Global Studies* 89, 90.
9 Ibrahim K Sundiata *Equatorial Guinea: colonialism, state terror, and the search for stability* (Routledge, 1990) 47.
10 As above.
11 With respect to this pressure, Sundiata observes that 'labor came from the most thickly populated areas of the Eastern Region. Thus, it was part of the more general Igbo diaspora that sent the Igbo and related peoples into northern Nigeria, Cameroon, and beyond'. See Sundiata (n 9) 47.
12 Margaret Peil 'The expulsion of West African aliens' (1971) 9(2) *The Journal of Modern African Studies* 205.
13 As above.
14 Olajide Aluko 'The expulsion of illegal aliens from Nigeria: a study in Nigeria's decision-making' (1985) 84(337) *African Affairs* 539–560.
15 As above, 551–552.
16 See Theresa Alfaro-Velcamp and Mark Shaw '"Please go home and build Africa": criminalizing immigrants in South Africa' (2016) 42(5) *Journal of Southern African Studies* 983–998.
17 Katharine M Donato and Donna Gabaccia *Gender and international migration: from the slavery era to the global age* (Russell Sage Foundation, 2015) 57.
18 The Revised Migration Policy Framework for Africa and Plan of Action (2018–2027), 5.
19 'Key migration terms' https://www.iom.int/key-migration-terms (accessed 25 August 2021).

20 Global Compact on Safe, Orderly and Regular Migration (2018).
21 As above, para 6.
22 As above, para 11.
23 As above, para 15(c).
24 As above, para 21.
25 Immigration Act (1963).
26 National Migration Policy (2015) 91.
27 As above, 8.
28 David James Cantor & Jacob O Apollo 'Internal displacement, internal migration and refugee flows: connecting the dots' (IDRP Research Briefing Paper, August 2020).
29 National Migration Policy (n 26), 49.
30 UN Refugee Convention Relating to the Status of Refugees (1951); Protocol Relating to the Status of Refugees (1967).
31 Article 8(2) of the OAU Refugee Convention Governing the Specific Aspects of Refugee Problems in Africa provides that: '[t]he present Convention shall be the effective regional complement in Africa of the 1951 United Nations Convention on the Status of Refugees'. See OAU Refugee Convention Governing the Specific Aspects of Refugee Problems in Africa (1969) (OAU 1969 Refugee Convention), art 8(2).
32 See 1951 UN Refugee Convention (n 30), art 1; OAU 1969 Refugee Convention (n 31), art 1(1).
33 OAU 1969 Refugee Convention (n 31), art 1(2).
34 National Commission for Refugees (Establishment, Etc.) Act 2004, art 1.
35 Kampala Convention (n 2), art 1(k).
36 For further discussion on the Nigerian Legal System, see generally Akintunde O Obilade *The Nigerian legal system* (Sweet and Maxwell, 1979).
37 The Constitution of the Federal Republic of Nigeria (1999), sec 1(3).
38 As above, secs 4(1) & (2) and 6, 7(a) & (b); Second Schedule to the Constitution (Part I & II).
39 As above, Second Schedule to the Constitution (Part I). the National Assembly is a bi-cameral legislative system comprising of a Senate and House of Representatives.
40 As above, Second Schedule to the Constitution (Part II).
41 *Attorney General of the Federation v Attorney-General of Lagos State* LPELR-20974 (SC) (2013), 150.
42 As above.
43 Such as in the domestication of treaties ratified by the country recognised in art 12(2) of the Constitution.
44 Convention on the Rights of the Child (1989); African Charter on the Rights and Welfare of the Child (1990); Child's Rights Act (2003).
45 The Constitution of the Federal Republic of Nigeria (n 37), sec 12(2).
46 The Constitution of the Federal Republic of Nigeria (n 37), sec 12(3).
47 The absence of concurrence from the states in the adoption of the CRA led to the delay in sub-national incorporation of the law. In nearly two decades, 25 states have adopted sub-national legislations. However, there are 11 states that are yet to adopt a legislation on the subject-matter. See '11 states yet to domesticate Child Rights Act – Minister' *Premium Times (Nigeria)* 13 October 2020.
48 Onyebuchi T Uwakah *Due process in Nigeria's administrative law system: history, current status and future* (University Press of America, 1997) 79–80.

49 *Njoku & Ors v Iheanatu & Ors* CA/PH/EPT/454/2007 (2008), 20–21.
50 Interpretation Act (1990), sec 37(1).
51 Interpretation Act (n 51), sec 18(1); *Yaki & Anor v Bagudu & Ors* LPELR-25721 (SC) (2015).
52 Section 46(3) of the Constitution provides that 'The Chief Justice of Nigeria may make rules with respect to the practice and procedure of a High Court for the purposes of this section.' The Constitution of the Federal Republic of Nigeria (n 37), art 46(3); Fundamental Rights (Enforcement Procedure) Rules (2009).
53 Fundamental Rights (Enforcement Procedure) Rules (n 52), Order II, Rule 1.
54 African Charter on Human and Peoples' Rights (1981).
55 *Master v Mansur & Ors* LPELR-23440 (CA) (2014), 23, paras D–F.
56 Uwakah (n 48) 85.
57 Interpretation Act (n 51), sec 32(1).
58 *Kalu v Odili & Ors* LPELR-1653 (SC) (1992), 41–42.
59 *Sheka v Bashari* LPELR-21403 (CA) (2013), 45.
60 *Nigeria Arab Bank Ltd v Barri Engineering Nig Ltd* LPELR-2007 (SC) (1995), 47–48.
61 See *Oni v Fayemi* NWLR (Pt 1089) 400 at 427–428 (2008)
62 *Omega Bank Plc v Government of Ekiti State* (2007) All FWLR (Pt. 386) 658 at 687–688.
63 *Nigeria Arab Bank Ltd v Barri Engineering Nig Ltd* (n 60).
64 Uwakah (n 48) 88.
65 *Oyewunmi & Anor v Ogunesan* LPELR-2880 (SC) (1990), 46; see also *Oseku v The Minister FCT, Abuja & Ors* LPELR-3560 (CA) (2007), 27.
66 *Nsirim v Nsirim* LPELR-8060 (SC) (2002).
67 *Yampa & Ors v Babareke & Anor* LPELR-41212 (CA) (2016).
68 Nonso Okafo *Reconstructing law and justice in a postcolony* (Routledge, 2016) 121; Chukwuma SA Okoli and Richard F Oppong *Private international law in Nigeria* (Hart Publishing, 2020) 335.
69 *Ojukwu v Agupusi & Anor* LPELR-22683 (CA) (2014), 42.
70 *Dada v State* (1977) NCLR 135.
71 *Pfizer Specialities Ltd v Chyzob Pharmacy Ltd* (2008) All FWLR (Pt. 414) 1455 at 1489, paras E–G; *Adetoun Oladeji (Nig) Ltd v Nigerian Breweries Plc* LPELR-160 (SC) (2007).
72 *Agbaje v Fashola* (2008) 6 NWLR (Pt 1082) 90 at 129, para. H.
73 *Ojukwu v Military Governor of Lagos State & Ors* CA/L/196/85 (1) (1985).
74 *Adedeji & Sons Motors Nigeria Limited v Immeh & Anor* LPELR-14104 (CA) (1996)
75 *Attorney General of the Federation v Attorney General of Lagos State* LPELR-20974 (SC) (2013), 97.
76 Vienna Convention on the Law of Treaties (1969), art 18.
77 See The Constitution of the Federal Republic of Nigeria (n 37), sec 12(1); *Abacha v Fawehinmi* (2000) LPELR-14 (SC).
78 See Vienna Convention on the Law of Treaties (n 76), art 26.
79 See Muyiwa Adigun 'The status of customary international law under the Nigerian legal system' (2019) 45(1) *Commonwealth Law Bulletin* 115–156; Elijah O Okebukola 'The application of international law in Nigeria and the façade of dualism' (2020) 11(1) *Nnamdi Azikwe University Journal of International Law and Jurisprudence* 15–28.
80 National Migration Policy (2015), para 3.1.

81 The Constitution of the Federal Republic of Nigeria (n 37), sec 17(2).
82 The Federal Executive council is the cabinet, and it comprises of the President, the Vice-President, and Ministers in charge of various federal government ministries.
83 'FEC approves new policy on IDPs' *Premium Times* 1 September 2021.
84 See Roberta Cohen and Francis M Deng (eds) *The forsaken people: case studies of the internally displaced* (Brookings Institution, 1998); Roberta Cohen and Francis M Deng *Masses in flight: the global crisis of internal displacement* (Brookings Institution Press, 1998).

2 Internal displacement in Nigeria

2.1 Introduction

This chapter examines the issue of internal displacement in Nigeria, describing this category of persons and considering the root causes of internal displacement in the country. The description of an internally displaced person (IDP) was a pertinent issue that emerged in the 1990s as a global standard on internal displacement was being discussed. What was clear was these persons were not refugees given that they remained within the borders of the state of their displacement. Adopting the refugee definition would also have been inadequate. While the Secretary-General provided an initial working description in an analytical report, there were inherent challenges with this, such as quantification, with the description of IDPs as persons moving suddenly in large numbers.[1] However, these concerns were subsequently resolved in the final text of the UN Guiding Principles on Internal Displacement (Guiding Principles) and reinforced in the African Union Convention for the Protection and Assistance of Internally Displaced Persons in Africa (Kampala Convention).[2] Within the legal definition in the Kampala Convention, this chapter examines the issue of internal displacement in Nigeria, reflecting on the definition and causes.

2.2 Definition

While it would appear that the description of an IDP is clear and does not raise any conceptual difficulty, a closer consideration of this definition unveils some questions integral to the furtherance of knowledge on an IDP.[3] For instance, what 'persons or groups of persons' entails may be quite straightforward if one considers the ordinary meaning of the word. However, the pertinent question is: does persons or groups include noncitizens of the country or is it restricted solely to citizens of a state? The pertinence of this question resonates from situations where migrants or

DOI: 10.4324/9781003146025-2

refugees are displaced and protection becomes an imperative for them. This pragmatic situation is not clearly emphasised in the description. However, there is nothing to suggest in the description that non-citizens are not contemplated. This is further reinforced by an emphasis on non-discrimination as a pertinent optic through which to advance protection.[4] Evidently, failing to include categories such as migrants and refugees in the context of protection in situations of internal displacement will go against the objective of protection and assistance in situations where internal displacement occurs.

Another pertinent dimension of this description is the notion of being 'forced or obliged to flee or to leave'.[5] While this notion clearly reinforces involuntary movement, there is a question as to whether a person who has left his home or place of habitual residence prior to a situation of internal displacement, but who cannot return, with the emergence of armed conflict or situations of generalised violence, for instance, will be considered an IDP. Placed within the Nigerian context, assuming a person leaves his/her home in a region of the country to go to another region prior to an attack by the Boko Haram insurgent group that creates a situation of internal displacement, and given the state of insecurity in the home region, that person cannot return home, can this person be considered an IDP? In the context of international refugee law, such situations create refugees *sur place*. However, this is not evident in the IDP context and the definition does not provide an indication as to whether such persons may arguably be regarded as such. However, there appears to be nothing that negates such an understanding, particularly given that the primary objective of the law on internal displacement is to protect persons from the effect of root causes of internal displacement, such as armed conflict or situations of generalised violence as in the scenario presented.

Moreover, another pertinent question in the IDP discussion is the issue of 'homes or places of habitual residence'. It might seem clear or straightforward that homes or places of habitual residence are places of abode; however, the complexity resonates from situations where displaced persons are squatters or nomadic pastoralists whose homes or places of habitual residence may not emerge as clearly as property rights holders or indigenous populations. This is not also clearly defined in the law on internal displacement. However, international law and the jurisprudence on internal displacement reflect the fact that understanding what constitutes 'places of habitual residence' needs to be construed in the context of more 'durable ties than mere residence';[6] however, this is not to be conflated with domicile. What is required, in essence, is 'residence of some standing or duration'.[7] However, the legality of such residence is not a necessity.

In the context of the description, another pertinent issue relates to the nature of the words 'in particular'. Evidently, the ordinary meaning of such words clearly expresses a specification.[8] However, the complexity of this definition resonates from the issue of whether it creates a closed list of root causes of internal displacement. Put differently, can it be assumed that the phrase 'in particular' categorically prescribes a conclusive list of instances that can occasion internal displacement? The pertinence of this question resonates from the fact that other root causes of internal displacement such as development projects are not specifically included within this description. While the description does not explicitly emphasise this point, a close look at this provision, and the fact that the law on internal displacement recognises other root causes of internal displacement such as development projects and climate change, clearly indicates that these causes are not excluded from the narrative on the basis of the words 'in particular'.

Another dimension of this definition relates to the root causes of internal displacement. There are four pertinent causes recognised in the description: 'armed conflict, generalized violence, natural or human-made disasters'.[9] While it would appear evident what these causes are, there is a question, for instance, as to the difference between armed conflict and generalised violence. Put differently, what is the threshold for armed conflict and how does it differ from instances of generalised violence? Moreover, there is a question of natural or human-made disasters and the difference or link between these two. Also, there are other root causes of internal displacement, the understanding of which is not explicit. For instance, what are development projects? Harmful practices? What is climate change and how do these issues relate to internal displacement? While the next section examines these root causes, it is pertinent to consider another dimension of this description. This dimension is the requirement that such persons 'have not crossed an internationally recognized state border'.

There are two major issues that emerge from this description. The first issue relates to the notion of statehood particularly for countries that may fulfil the criteria on statehood under the Montevideo Convention on the Rights and Duties of States;[10] however, there is the political question of international recognition. Within the African context, such issues resonate from the Somalia and Somaliland context. Moreover, there is also a second issue regarding the requirement that such person 'have not crossed an internationally recognized state border'.[11] The question this raises is: what happens in situations where an IDP perhaps crosses the border of state A into another state B and then crosses back into the state of displacement (A)? Placed within the Nigerian context, for instance, what happens if a person displaced from a Nigerian town along its border with Chad or Niger crosses into either of these countries and then back into Nigeria? Evidently, it would appear that in such instances, that individual would have crossed an internationally recognised state border; however, will such person be an

IDP for the purpose of the legal description upon return to Nigeria? The definition does not provide clarity. Neither do other provisions in the law on internal displacement. However, there is nothing in the definition that presupposes that where a person crosses from state A to another state B and back to state A, such person may not be regarded as an IDP. Evidently, such interpretation will defeat the purpose of protection. What is essential is that such displaced person is within the border of the state of displacement for the purpose of inclusion in protection and assistance.

2.3 Causes

The description of an IDP unveils certain root causes of internal displacement, although it does not categorically encompass all causes and does not exclude the possibility of a list of other root causes of internal displacement. Specifically, in the description, there are four root causes: 'armed conflict, situations of generalized violence, violations of human rights or natural or human-made disasters'.[12] In understanding these root causes, it is relevant to examine what these various causes mean and how they manifest within the Nigerian context. For the purpose of discussion, this section is divided into two parts: definition-specific root causes and non-definition-specific root causes. Under definition-specific root causes, the four pertinent causes mentioned in the definition of internal displacement are examined. Following this, other root causes of internal displacement that are not specifically incorporated in the definition, but which emerge from other provisions of the law on internal displacement, will be considered.

2.3.1 Definition-specific root causes

This section examines the various root causes of internal displacement that are explicitly emphasised in the definition of an IDP. As earlier emphasised, these include: 'armed conflict, situations of generalized violence, violations of human rights or natural or human-made disasters'.[13]

2.3.1.1 Armed conflict

To understand armed conflict, it is pertinent to reflect on the laws of war and the jurisprudential expositions from international criminal courts that expound on armed conflicts and situations that will qualify as such. The jurisprudence of two international mechanisms: the International Criminal Tribunal of the former Yugoslavia (ICTY) and the International Criminal Tribunal for Rwanda (ICTR) offer a significant basis on which to understand what armed conflict implies.[14] From the jurisprudence of both courts, there are certain definitional criteria for an armed conflict. First, armed conflicts are 'hostilities', 'resort to armed force' or 'protracted armed violence'. Where an armed conflict is between two states, the rules of the international laws of war (or international humanitarian law) applies. Such armed conflict between two states is generally regarded as an international armed conflict. And this is clear and well-settled. However, the pertinent issue relates to conflicts between states and non-state actors which non-international armed conflict covers. Put differently, what is the benchmark or criteria for a particular conflict to qualify as a non-international armed conflict?

Generally, in the laws of war,[15] non-international armed conflicts are determined in relation to the organisation of the armed group and the intensity of the conflict.[16] However, the Rome Statute of the International Criminal Court (ICC) appears to include a third criterion which is the element of 'protraction'.[17] However, it has been the practice of courts to interpret the notion of protraction in relation to the element of intensity of the conflict rather than as a separate criterion within the context of determining the existence of a situation of non-international armed conflict. This position is reinforced in the *Prosecutor v Ramush Haradinaj, Idriz Balaj and Lahi Brahimaj*.[18] Moreover, Additional Protocol II sets a higher standard for understanding non-international armed conflict providing the material scope of the instrument as between states:[19]

> armed forces and dissident armed forces or other organized armed groups which, under responsible command, exercise such control over a part of its territory as to enable them to carry out sustained and concerted military operations and to implement this Protocol.

This material scope introduces four criteria. First, the parties to the conflict are states versus dissident armed forces or states versus other organised armed groups. The challenge of this description is that it tends to exclude situations where armed groups may be at war with themselves, for instance, in a failed state. Such situations clearly will seem to fall outside the material scope of Additional Protocol II.

The second dimension relates to the notion of 'organisation' of an armed group. When will an armed group be said to be organised? In the *Prosecutor v Ljube Boškoski and Johan Tarčulovski*, five main criteria were put forward by the ICTY, namely: a command structure, the ability of the armed group to conduct operations, a level of logistics operations, the existence of internal disciplinary measures and the ability of the armed group 'to speak with one voice'.[20] While these indications are imperative, they appear to impose a strict criteria, one which a significant number of armed groups operating in modern asymmetric warfare may not meet. However, the ICRC has tended to adopt a fairly relaxed approach emphasising 'a minimum of organisation'. For this, it would appear that armed groups have to be 'under a certain command structure and have the capacity to sustain military operations'.[21]

A third criterion is the notion of responsible command. The doctrine of command responsibility presupposes the existence of superiors that regulate the activities of subordinates in a given context. Based on this doctrine, superiors are accountable for breaches of the laws of war by subordinates under their 'effective authority and control'[22] where they knew or should have known of such acts and failed to 'take all necessary and reasonable measures within his or her power to prevent or repress their commission or to submit the matter to the competent authorities for investigation and prosecution'.[23] In the case of the *Prosecutor v Jean-Pierre Bemba Gombo*, the International Criminal Court expatiated on this doctrine.[24] In this case, Bemba was accused of crimes against humanity committed in the Central Republic of Congo by the Movement for the Liberation of Congo which he led. The Trial Chamber upheld the responsibility of Mr Bemba for these crimes, reinforcing the fact that the duty to 'take all necessary and reasonable measures … rests upon his possession of effective authority and control'.[25] The Trial Chamber was of the opinion that what matters is not an 'explicit legal capacity' but rather a 'material ability to act'.[26] As such, 'what constitutes "all reasonable and necessary measures within his or her power" shall be assessed on the basis of the de jure and/or de facto power of the commander and the exercise he or she makes of this power'.[27] Considering the various measures which Mr Bemba could have taken including the withdrawal of his troops from the Central African Republic,[28] the Trial Chamber concluded that 'the measures Mr Bemba did take patently fell short of "all necessary and reasonable measures" to prevent and repress the commission of crimes within his material ability'.[29]

However, on appeal, the Appeals Chamber reversed the decision of the Trial Chamber. In expounding on the doctrine of command responsibility, the Appeals Chamber emphasised that the provision of article 28 of the Rome Statute, which incorporates the doctrine of command responsibility 'requires commanders to do what is necessary and *reasonable* under the circumstances'.[30] The Appeals Chamber was of the view that the Trial Chamber 'paid insufficient attention to the fact that the MLC troops were operating in a foreign country with the attendant difficulties on Mr Bemba's ability, as a remote commander, to take measures'.[31] Consequently, the Appeals Chamber found the Trial Chamber in error and as such emphasised, among others, that

> the Trial Chamber's failure to fully appreciate the limitations that Mr Bemba would have faced in investigating and prosecuting crimes as a

remote commander sending troops to a foreign country had an important impact on the overall assessment of the measures taken by Mr Bemba.[32]

The Appeals Chamber further emphasised that if the Trial Chamber had 'properly assessed the measures that Mr Bemba took'[33] and 'properly considered the list of measures that it stated that Mr Bemba could have taken in light of the limitations that he faced in the specific circumstances in which he was operating',[34] a different conclusion might have emerged.

This decision has generated a rich flurry of debates as, among other things, it appears to introduce a novel standard of 'remoteness', and as such appears to create two different standards for commanders in close proximity to their subordinates and those that are not in close proximity, with the latter seemingly having a lesser degree of responsibility. However, with the evolving nature of modern warfare, there is a question as to the implication of this decision particularly with the emergence of technology and the fact that the concept of remoteness in itself is relative. Judge Eboe-Osuji, while delivering a concurring judgement, seemed to be mindful of this, emphasising that[35]

> I would not subscribe to any interpretation of the Majority Opinion as suggesting that the geographic remoteness of a commander is a factor all of its own, which would necessarily insulate him from criminal responsibility. Geographic remoteness is only a factor to be considered among other circumstances or peculiarities of a given case. It serves its greatest value in the assessment of what is *reasonable* as a measure to prevent or repress violations to submit them to competent authorities for investigation and prosecution. It is noted, in this connection, that the obligation is not to do *all* that is *conceivable* and necessary, considered from hindsight. It is, rather, to do *all* that is *reasonable* and necessary – no doubt in the circumstances at the time.

Increasingly, with the ability of superiors to operate effectively while being remote, a re-calibration of this position may, invariably emerge. But whether remote or otherwise, responsible command, as a third criterion, exists where there are superiors that reinforce hierarchical leadership within an armed group.

A fourth criterion under Additional Protocol II is the issue that an armed group must exercise control over territory. There is a question that emerges from this rhetoric as to what is implied by the exercise of control over territory. Put differently, does this imply that an armed group needs to exercise control in terms of geographic expanse or does it imply a qualitative control in terms of value or quality of such control? A consideration of the provision of Additional Protocol II seems to lean towards the fact that the essence of control should be towards enabling such armed groups to 'carry out sustained and concerted military operations and to implement this Protocol',[36] and as such qualitative control is envisaged. According to Sivakumaran, '[t]erritorial control is, then, an enabling element, one that demonstrates the ability of the armed group. It is a qualitative issue rather than a quantitative one'.[37] In the *Prosecutor v Jean Paul Akayesu*, this resonates in the jurisprudence of the ICTR that[38]

> armed forces must be able to dominate a sufficient part of the territory so as to maintain sustained and concerted military operations and to apply Additional Protocol II. In essence, the operations must be continuous and planned. The territory in their control is usually that which has eluded the control of the government forces.

Having established the criteria for understanding non-international armed conflict and situations in which Additional Protocol II will apply, a pertinent question that resonates is whether the *Jama'atu Ahlis Sunna Lidda'awali wal-Jihad* (also known as Boko Haram) is a non-international armed conflict.[39] Answering the first part of the question necessitates a consideration of whether Boko Haram is an organised armed group and if there is intensity of the conflict. In 2013, the Office of the Prosecutor (OTP) recognised that[40]

> there is a reasonable basis to believe that since July 2009, Boko Haram has committed the following acts constituting crimes against humanity: (i) murder under article 7(1)(a) and (ii) persecution under article 7(1)(h) of the Statute. In particular, the information available provides a reasonable basis to believe that since July 2009 Boko Haram has launched a widespread and systematic attack that has resulted in the killing of more than 1,200 Christian and Muslims civilians in different locations throughout Nigeria, including Borno, Yobe, Katsina, Kaduna, Bauchi, Gombe and Kano States in the North as well as Abuja, Kaduna and Plateau States in Central Nigeria. The consistent pattern of such incidents indicates that the group possesses the means to carry out a widespread and/or systematic attack, and displays internal coordination and organizational control required to that end.

However, the OTP's report fell short of categorising the situation as a non-international armed conflict at the time, given the need for more evidence. But over the last decade, significant evidence has emerged with respect to the organisational structure of the group. In 2015, Boko Haram pledged support to ISIS. While its operation is highly decentralised, the organisational structure consists of a Shura Council which is the highest decision-making body. The Shura Council is headed by the leader of the group (also known as the *Amir ul-Aam*). Estimates of the number of members of the Council have been placed at 30.[41] This Council approves tactical operations, although in recent years, the leader of the group has consolidated much of this power.[42] Since the group's inception and over the last decade, the hostilities between the state and Boko Haram has increased. The group engages in military operations with sophisticated weapons: mortar bombs, drones, improved explosive devices (IEDs) and rocket-propelled grenades. Aside from significant military sophistication and territorial control, more than two million people have been displaced by the activities of the armed group.[43] The growing onslaught of the group has led to the establishment of a Multinational Joint Task Force (MNJTF) involving the armed forces of Nigeria, Niger, Cameroon, Chad and Benin.[44] Evidently, the fact that the Boko Haram insurgency is a non-international armed conflict has also been recognised by the International Committee of the Red Cross (ICRC).[45] In the context of this conflict, common article 3 of the Geneva Convention evidently applies.

However, there is a pertinent question as to whether Additional Protocol II specifically on the protection of civilians in non-international armed conflict applies. As earlier emphasised, there are four criteria established for the application of this instrument. Effectively, it is clear that the armed conflict is primarily between the armed forces of the Nigerian state and Boko Haram, although there are other states in the Lake Chad region involved individually and through the MNJTF.[46] Second, the organisation of the group has been established.[47] Moreover, it is evident that there is responsible command. But a pertinent question is whether Boko Haram exercises control over territory. Evidently, this has emerged through a plethora of reports reflecting the qualitative dimension and the fact that they effectively control parts of the north-eastern region of Nigeria.[48] And while the government, through its armed forces and the MNJTF, has made strides towards reclaiming parts of the territory held by Boko Haram, there is a constant cycle in the armed conflict that witnesses Boko Haram gain less territory at some point and more at other times, with the bottom line being that territories are still being controlled by Boko Haram. A similar argument can be made for the splinter group – Islamic State of West Africa Province (ISWAP), an offshoot of Boko Haram, also with an allegiance to ISIS, motioned on a similar agenda of establishing a caliphate.[49] The provisions of Additional Protocol II apply in both instances to the protection of civilian populations, particularly the millions of individuals displaced. However, actual compliance with these norms is a significantly different narrative.

2.3.1.2 Generalised violence

Situations of generalised violence are a broad category of violence perpetuated as acts of terror against a population within a state. In the Nigerian context, such a situation ranges from inter-ethnic clashes to electoral violence. This form of violence is often indiscriminate and may involve both state and non-state actors. Generalised violence broadly includes violence that does not fall within the context of armed conflict given the required threshold. Much of the discussion on this issue has emerged within the Latin American context of gang violence in countries including Colombia and the Northern Triangle.[50] This violence resonates from a breakdown in law and order and prevalent institutional crises within states. This violence is also precipitated by unemployment and governance deficits. In regions where there are socio-economic disparities and poverty levels are high, the onset of this form of violence is rife. While these are latent spaces for the conflict to grow, there are also other contexts in which this violence emerges, such as in situations where xenophobic tendencies emerge, or where there is general dissatisfaction with governance or in situations where there are ethnic or religious tensions among groups within society. This form of violence could also emerge from the absence of adequate social cohesion measures or political divisions stemming from populist narratives. While this form of violence includes a broad range of issues, four dimensions are discussed in this section. These are: gang violence, violent extremism, electoral violence and intercommunal clashes.

Gang violence has emerged as a significant challenge in parts of Nigeria. In the early 2000s, much of these activities emerged from the prevalent marginalisation in the southern-oil producing states and the demands for control of resource revenues.[51] However, in recent years, activities of indiscriminate terror by gangs in some parts of the country have been recorded.[52] In July 2019, Reuters reported that[53]

> armed gangs have killed hundreds of people in northwest Nigeria this year and forced at least 20,000 to flee to neighbouring Niger, adding to security problems in a country also struggling with an Islamist insurgency in the northeast and clashes between farmers and herders in central states.

By September 2019, the UN High Commissioner for Refugees reported that over '40,000 people have now been forced to cross from northwest Nigeria into Niger', premised on the indiscriminate attacks of armed gangs.[54] Severally described in the news as 'motorcycle gang' and 'armed bandits',[55] these groups have become a significant menace in various parts of the state.[56] There are also violent extremisms although much of this is cast against the activities of Boko Haram and ISWAP which are active armed conflict situations in the state. However, there are emerging factions of extremism founded on radical ideologies and in the latent state of operations for which significant attention is required given their ability to instigate generalised violence and consequently, situations of internal displacement.[57]

Moreover, another prevalent form of generalised violence is electoral violence. Following Nigeria's independence in 1960, this form of violence emerged from the political rivalry in the western region between the Action Group and the Nigerian National Democratic Party over the control of the Western Assembly.[58] Over the last six decades, there have been significant pockets of violence in electoral processes during the second (1979–1983), third (1992–1993) and fourth republics (1999–present).[59] Intercommunal clashes have also become a significant precipitant of displacement in Nigeria. There are two dimensions of these clashes – ethno-religious clashes and the pastoralist-agrarian conflict. Much of the discussion on the first dimension of these clashes has centred around occurrences in the Kaduna region since the 1980s and in Plateau since 2001.[60] Moreover, there have been similar clashes in other parts of the country including Adamawa and Kwara.[61] With regards to clashes between pastoralists and agrarian communities, notably in the middle belt region, the situation in Benue is most prominent with the displacement of tens of thousands of people in the region.

2.3.1.3 Violations of human rights

Human rights violations as a root cause of internal displacement encompass a wide range of issues relating to civil, political and socio-economic rights.[62] As a catch-all lens through which to consider various forms of internal displacement concerns, this root cause leverages on human rights norms that are well-established and that enjoy popular support in national, regional and global normative contexts. At the Nigerian national level, there is also significant support for human rights norms reflected both in the Constitution and in a plethora of national legislations and policies. Moreover, this root cause of internal displacement is important given the fact that the idea of human rights reinforce obligations on states: such obligation being quadripartite: respect, promote, protect and fulfil.[63] Where these obligations are not actualised, their impacts may have far-reaching implications and extend to internal displacement consequences. Moreover, there is a responsibility on non-state actors to respect human rights reinforced under international human rights law. Such existing narratives serve as a lens for defining the roles of various actors and considering if such roles have been advanced in the prevention of internal displacement. Understanding internal displacement from the perspective of human rights violations provides an insight into the discourse on the protection of various groups of persons whose rights are reinforced under international human rights law including women, children, persons with disabilities and older persons. Moreover, there is also the imperative that understanding internal displacement from the perspective of human rights violations leverages on well-established jurisprudential knowledge at various levels of governance with the existence of specific mechanisms such as treaty bodies. Understanding violations of human rights in the context of internal displacement also reinforces the pertinence of non-discrimination, which is principal to the furtherance of prevention of internal displacement and protection of IDPs. Much of what culminates into situations of internal displacement derives from existing marginalisation and the use of power in a dimension that prejudices the interest of specific populations. For instance, in situations where women are subjected to gender-based violence, such rhetoric often stems from the prevalence of discrimination against women within societies. Moreover, such may also be the case for persons with disabilities (PWDs) or older persons.

Within the Nigerian context, internal displacement as a consequence of human rights violations has significantly been linked to other root causes of internal displacement. This is due to the fact that a fundamental premise upon which a plethora of these issues emerges relates to violations of human rights. Moreover, a significant dimension through which this also resonates is forced evictions.[64] This has been an evident problem in various parts of the country with rapid urbanisation and political persuasions towards economic growth and development. Significantly, violations of human rights as a root cause of internal displacement creates an organic descriptive field for contextualising situations of internal displacement.

2.3.1.4 Natural or human-made disasters

Natural or human-made disasters are situations of internal displacement that often reflect large-scale catastrophic events. This form of internal displacement relates to a wide range of events that seriously affect societies as a whole. In the Draft Articles on the Protection of Persons in the Event of Disasters, the International Law Commission defines disasters as 'a calamitous event or series of events resulting in widespread loss of life, great human suffering and distress, mass displacement, or large-scale material or environmental damage, thereby seriously disrupting the functioning of society'.[65] Over the last decade, natural or human-made disasters have become a significant root cause of internal displacement globally. Within this context, natural disasters include hurricanes, cyclones and torrential rainfalls.

In the Nigerian context, this form of disaster is mostly reflected in torrential rainfalls. Significant displacement of populations has also emerged from this context. For instance, in 2018, the National Emergency Management Authority observed that more than 600,000 people were reportedly displaced by torrential rainfall.[66] Human-made disasters such as nuclear explosions, industrial accidents and oil spills have also resulted in significant population displacement in various parts of the world. In Nigeria, the discussion on human-made disasters has mostly emerged from the Niger Delta context with situations of natural resource extraction and its consequential impacts on the livelihood of several communities.[67] One of the dimensions of impact is displacement.[68]

However, a significant intersection between natural and human-made disasters is the growing concern on the issue of climate change. This is not specifically recognised in the Guiding Principles; however, the issue of climate change resonates from the Kampala Convention as a root cause of internal displacement.[69]

While the next section examines this issue in more detail, it is relevant to discuss climate change as a link between natural and human-made disasters. Under the Paris Agreement, countries recognise the fact that 'climate change is a common concern of humankind' and as such it is important to foster 'engagement of all levels of government and various actors'.[70] Climate change may be loosely defined as an increase in the global average surface temperature.[71] This temperature has significantly increased over the last decades due to the effects of anthropogenic activities with the concentration of greenhouse gases into the atmosphere, significant among which is carbon dioxide. According to the Intergovernmental Panel on Climate Change (IPCC), '[h]uman-induced warming reached approximately $1°C$ (likely between $0.8°C$ and $1.2°C$) above pre-industrial levels in 2017, increasing at $0.2°C$ (likely between $0.1°C$ and $0.3°C$) per decade (*high confidence*)'.[72]

In the last couple of years, the increase in global average temperatures has had a plethora of impacts in various parts of the world: on food security, adequate standards of living and the realisation of sustainable development.[73] Population displacement is also a pertinent dimension of this impact. The World Bank reports that by 2050, more than 143 million people will move internally within state borders and of this figure, 86 million people will be in sub-Saharan Africa.[74] While this figure incorporates both migrants and displaced populations, it reflects a significant crisis underway if global trends are not reversed. In the Paris Agreement, countries agreed to limit global average temperature to '1.5°C above pre-industrial levels'.[75] However, there have been significant concerns about reaching this target in view of global trends in climate emissions and differentiated perspectives among states on the imperative for adopting urgent solutions in order to effectively reverse climate impacts.

2.3.2 *Non-definition-specific root causes*

There are root causes of internal displacement that, while not included in the IDP definition,[76] are referenced in the other parts of the global and regional frameworks on internal displacement and are of relevance in the Nigerian context. This section examines three root causes – climate change, development projects and harmful practices. This section discusses these root causes of internal displacement with specific reference to Nigeria.

2.3.2.1 *Climate change*

Increasingly, the impact of climate change on populations from the point of displacement is becoming a concern.[77] There are four dimensions of the nexus between climate change and internal displacement: slow onset disasters, sudden onset disasters, climate-development induced displacement and the climate-conflict nexus.

Sudden onset disasters are rapid cataclysmic incidences such as torrential rainfalls and cyclones. These disasters often drive the narrative on climate displacement and have become a prevalent lens for understanding the effect of climate change. Increasingly, this nexus is being drawn in evidence-based research linking heavy precipitations in the southern region of the country to climate change.[78] Oladipo notes that precipitation is expected to increase in the southern savanna region of the country 'by approximately 5–20%'.[79] In a study on annual rainfall incidence in Nigeria between 1981–2015, Ogunrinde et al. observe an increase in rainfall patterns, validating the point made by the IPCC that 'coastal areas (south) will experience more rainfall in the 21st century, which might lead to flooding, while the Sahel region will have more drought occurrences'.[80]

Aside from sudden onset disasters, the growing imperative for addressing climate change through adaptation and mitigation projects has also become a concern in various parts of the continent given the potential impact on populations within the scope of these projects. While research in this area is few and far between, there have been concerns regarding the execution of such projects in several parts of the continent such as the Democratic Republic of Congo, Senegal and Uganda.[81] In Nigeria, for instance, this emerged in the context of a REDD+ initiative which was sought to be carried out in Cross River state.[82] However, this project was resisted by local communities given the absence of adequate compensation, consultation and information on the project. Moreover, the fact that these projects will affect the economic livelihood of the communities within its reach led to its resistance.

Slow onset disasters are gradual incidents that occur over a period of time and as such are not immediate in effect. These forms of disasters include sea-level rise, desertification and drought. Induced by the pace of climate change, there are emerging episodes of droughts in parts of Nigeria, notably in the regions of the Sahel. According to Haider,[83]

> Climate change is exacerbating drought and aridity, affecting the entire savanna landscape of Northern Nigeria and resulting in a decline of socio-economic activities around Lake Chad. The Northeast and the Northwest are the most vulnerable. The combination of rising heat and less rain has hastened desert encroachment, with loss of the wetlands, and fast reduction in the amount of surface water, flora and fauna resources on land

The onset of this form of disaster in the northern region increasingly induces the north-south movement of pastoralist populations, the ripple effect of which is another dimension of the climate change and internal displacement nexus – the pastoralist-agrarian conflict.[84] This dimension of displacement, which also resonates in the context of generalised violence, has emerged as a significant concern in Nigeria. Due to these conflicts, thousands of individuals have been displaced.[85] In 2017, the International Committee of the Red Cross (ICRC) observed that in the middle belt region 'continued clashes between farmers and herdsmen displaced more than 130,000 people from Benue, Kaduna, Nasarawa and Taraba states alone'.[86]

2.3.2.2 Development projects

The need to economically position countries for the furtherance of economic growth has significantly driven development projects in many parts of the continent, including Nigeria.[87] However, this drive towards economic growth has often come at a significant human cost.[88] In many parts of Nigeria, development-induced displacement (DID) has become a significant concern with the emergence of large dams, resource extraction, urban renewal, agricultural investments and climate projects, discussed in the previous section. These projects are often legitimate in driving national processes towards enhanced economic growth; however, the fact that their implementation is often done without due regard to their consequences on the livelihood of affected populations creates a significant challenge, one which has become an issue in the context of internal displacement. That these projects are often characterised by inadequate compensation, consultation and information create dire consequences – consequences which raises questions regarding the narrative of development as a one-sided endeavour which does not incorporate everyone within society. Since the 1960s, there has been a plethora of these issues, mostly reflected through the various dam projects in several parts of the country.

In the context of dams, the situation of the Kainji, Tiga and Dadin Kowa dams are significant paradigms. The construction of the Kainji dam led to the displacement of more than 40,000 individuals.[89] While resettlement was initiated, the houses given to the displaced populations were not adequate and did not sufficiently reflect the household sizes of those displaced.[90] Moreover, a similar issue emerged from the Tiga dam which was constructed in the 1970s and which led to the displacement of at least 13,000 individuals.[91] Those displaced were taken to regions that were less fertile than their former places of residence and away from water sources pertinent to the furtherance of their livelihood.[92] Moreover, there were also concerns with respect to the Dadin Kowa dam of the 1980s with the displaced receiving little support in displacement.[93] These issues are also reflective of the challenges experienced in the context of DID within a much broader African society where electrification for economic development drives the construction of large dams at the expense of affected populations.

These issues have also emerged in the context of resource extraction, particularly in the Niger Delta region. In this region, population displacements have been the effect of resource extraction and environmental degradation. In the literature, much of the discussion has centred around oil spills in the Niger Delta. However, there have also been incidences of displacement for the furtherance of actual projects and expansion of existing ones. For instance, in the periods between February to April 2005, houses belonging to villagers in a town in Port-Harcourt were demolished to make way for an oil expansion initiative by the Nigerian AGIP Oil Company 'despite strong opposition from residents' group and human rights organizations including the Movement for the Survival of the Ogoni People (MOSOP)'.[94] Similar concerns have also emerged in other contexts of resource extraction. However, not much research has emerged in this regard, i.e., with respect to other natural resource extractions such as the extraction of gold and lead.

In recent years, however, the most prominent form of internal displacement due to development projects in Nigeria is reflected in urban renewal projects.[95] Across various parts of the country, this reflects in the manner in which waterfront dwellers and peri-urban residents are being displaced in various states including Lagos, Abuja and Rivers. For the Abuja Master Plan, more than 800,000 people were displaced in the periods between 2003 and 2007.[96] In a 2012 report, Spaces for Change reported that homes were demolished 'without adequate prior notice, without adequate consultation with affected persons, without payment of compensation or provision of alternate shelter, rendering several families ... homeless'.[97] Similar issues have also characterised population displacement in states of the federation such as Lagos and Rivers where 'governments have forcibly removed people from informal settlements built on land earmarked for development projects'.[98] Examples of these, for instance, resonates in the displacement of more than 20,000 people from waterfront communities in River State for the Greater Port-Harcourt City Development Plan and at least, 30,000 people belonging to the Otodo-Gbame community in Lagos state.[99]

Agricultural investments projects have also emerged as a significant concern. A pertinent case in point is with the Diamond Farms project in Taraba state.[100] This project emerged from a G8 New Alliance for Food Security and Nutrition in Africa.[101] With the objective of growing food to enhance agricultural production, the Taraba state government approved the project, however, this was without adequate consultation with local farmers. It was observed that these farmers 'were never asked if they agreed to the project or under what terms they would accept the project, and were thus kept out of a decision that has major impacts on their lives'.[102] These narratives have also been prevalent in various parts of the continent where governments seek to transition economies through modernised agriculture and as such enhance productivity through foreign investments. In the process of achieving these economic goals, lands belonging to local communities are often taken in the exercise of eminent domain without adequate processes of compensation, consultation and information. Consequently, local communities, whose livelihood capacities are linked to access to lands and subsistence modes of production, are left impoverished.

2.3.2.3 Harmful practices

One of the least discussed root causes of internal displacement is the issue of harmful practices.[103] These practices relate to 'all behaviour, attitudes and/or practices which negatively affect the fundamental rights of women and girls, such as their right to life, health, dignity, education and physical integrity'.[104] That harmful practices are occasioning displacement, however, is a rhetoric that is not often discussed, in part, given the need for evidence on the linkage between such practices and internal displacement. However, a pertinent dimension in which the nexus between harmful practices and internal displacement resonates in Nigeria is in the area of child marriage. Statistics indicate that 44% of girls are given away in marriage in Nigeria before the age of 18 and about 18% before their 15th birthday.[105] This practice is mostly predicated on religion and socio-economic inequalities. In the northern region of the country, the practice of child marriage is further exacerbated by the Boko Haram insurgency where 'desperate parents increasingly see early marriage as a way to protect their daughters as fighting closes schools, and families grow more impoverished'.[106] However, evidence has begun to emerge of girls fleeing this practice, particularly in this region.[107]

2.4 Conclusion

While much of the discussion on internal displacement in Nigeria has been with respect to the issue of armed conflict, there are evidently other root causes that have occasioned significant population displacement. In the description contained in IDP frameworks, some of these root causes, in addition to armed conflict, include generalised violence, violation of human rights and natural or human-made disasters. However, there are also other root causes not explicitly contained in the description such as climate change, development projects and harmful practices. Across the country, these root causes have been evident. Given the prevalence of these root causes and the attendant vulnerabilities of IDPs in these contexts, having norms that respond adequately to the protection and assistance of IDPs in the country is important. The next chapter examines the normative regime on internal displacement in Nigeria.

Notes

1 Paragraph 17 of the Analytical Report of the Secretary-General on Internally Displaced Persons provides that 'the term "internally displaced persons" will be used to refer to persons who have been forced to flee their homes suddenly or unexpectedly in large numbers; as a result of armed conflict, internal strife, systematic violations of human rights or natural or man-made disasters; and who are within the territory of their own country'. UN Commission on Human Rights, *Analytical Report of the Secretary-General on Internally Displaced Persons*, UN Doc E/CN.4/1992/23 (1992), para 17.

2 African Union Convention for the Protection and Assistance of Internally Displaced Persons in Africa (23 October 2009) (Kampala Convention); Stephanie Ojeda 'The Kampala Convention on internally displaced persons: some international humanitarian law aspects' (2010) 29(3) *Refugee Survey Quarterly* 58; Prisca Kamungi 'Beyond good intentions: implementing the Kampala Convention' (2010) 34 *Forced Migration Review* 53; Maria Stavropoulou 'The Kampala Convention and protection from arbitrary displacement' (2010) 36 *Forced Migration Review* 62; Katinka Ridderbos 'The Kampala Convention and obligations of armed groups' (2011) 37 *Forced Migration Review* 36; Flavia Z Guistiniani 'New hopes and challenges for the protection of IDPs in Africa: the Kampala Convention for the Protection and Assistance of Internally Displaced Persons in Africa' (2011) 39(2) *Denver Journal of International Law and Policy* 347; Lauren Groth 'Engendering

protection: an analysis of the 2009 Kampala Convention and its provision for internally displaced women' (2011) 23(2) *International Journal of Refugee Law* 221; Allehone M Abebe 'The Kampala Convention and environmentally induced displacement in Africa', IOM Intersessional Workshop on Climate Change, Environmental Degradation and Migration, Geneva, Switzerland (29–30 March 2011); Mehari T Maru 'The Kampala Convention and its contribution in filling the protection gap in international law' (2011) 1(1) *Journal of Internal Displacement* 91; Cristiano D'Orsi 'Strengths and weaknesses in the protection of the internally displaced persons in Sub-Saharan Africa' (2012) 28(1) *Connecticut Journal of International Law* 73; Laurence Juma 'The narrative of vulnerability and deprivation in protection regimes for the internally displaced persons (IDPs) in Africa: an appraisal of the Kampala Convention' (2012) 16 *Law, Democracy and Development* 219; Mehari T Maru *The Kampala Convention and its contribution to international law: legal analyses and interpretations of the African Union Convention for the Protection and Assistance of Internally Displaced Persons* (Eleven Publishing, 2014); Moetsi Duchatellier and Catherine Phuong 'The African contribution to the protection of internally displaced persons: a commentary on the 2009 Kampala Convention' in Vincent Chetail and Céline Bauloz (eds) *Research handbook on international law and migration* (Edward Elgar, 2014) 650; Dan Kuwali 'From durable solutions to holistic solutions: prevention of displacement in Africa' (2014) 6(2/3) *African Journal of Legal Studies* 265; Leslie C Bailey 'Out of Africa: toward regional solutions for internal displacement' (2014) 39(1) *Brooklyn Journal of International Law* 353; Allehone M Abebe *The emerging law on forced migration in Africa: development and implementation of the Kampala Convention on internal displacement* (Routledge, 2016); Amare Tesfaye 'Internally displaced persons in Africa: a glimpse view of the protections accorded in the Kampala Convention' (2017) 9 *Jimma University Journal of Law* 1; Adama Dieng 'Protecting internally displaced: the value of the Kampala Convention as a regional example' (2017) 99(904) *International Review of the Red Cross* 263–282; Romola Adeola *Development-induced displacement and human rights in Africa: the Kampala Convention* (Routledge, 2020).

3 For a discussion of this issue, please see: Romola Adeola *The internally displaced person in international law* (Edward Elgar, 2020).

4 The Kampala Convention mandate states to: 'Respect and ensure respect and protection of the human rights of internally displaced persons, including humane treatment, non- discrimination, equality and equal protection of law'. See Kampala Convention (n 2), art 3(1)(d).

5 Kampala Convention (n 2), art 1(k).

6 Adeola (n 3) 11.

7 Atle Grahl-Madsen *The status of refugees in international law: refugee character* (AW Sijthoff, 1966).

8 Walter Kälin 'Guiding Principles on Internal Displacement: annotations' Studies in Transnational Legal Policy No 38, The American Society of International Law (2008) 4.

9 Kampala Convention (n 2), art 1(k).

10 Montevideo Convention on the Rights and Duties of States (1933).

11 Kampala Convention (n 2), art 1(k).

12 As above.

13 As above.

14 *The Prosecutor v Duško Tadić* International Criminal Tribunal of the Former Yugoslavia, Appeals Chamber (IT-94-1-AR72) (2 October 1995); *The Prosecutor v Jean Paul Akayesu* International Criminal Tribunal for Rwanda, Trial Chamber 1 (ICTR-96-4-T) (2 September 1998).

15 Geneva Convention for the Amelioration of the Condition of the Wounded and Sick in Armed Forces in the Field (12 August 1949); Geneva Convention for the Amelioration of the Condition of Wounded, Sick and Shipwrecked Members of Armed Forces at Sea (12 August 1949); Geneva Convention Relative to the Treatment of Prisoners of War (12 August 1949); Geneva Convention Relative to the Protection of Civilian Persons in Time of War (12 August 1949); Protocol Additional to the Geneva Conventions of 12 August 1949 and Relating to the Protection of Victims of International Armed Conflict (8 June 1977); Protocol Additional to the Geneva Conventions of 12 August 1949 and Relating to the Protection of Victims of Non-international Armed Conflict (Additional Protocol II) (8 June 1977).

16 See Anthony Cullen *The concept of non-international armed conflict in international humanitarian law* (Cambridge University Press, 2010); Sandesh Sivakumaran *The law of non-international armed conflict* (Oxford University Press, 2012); Yoram Dinstein *Non-international armed conflicts in international law* (Cambridge University Press, 2014); Eric David 'Internal (non-international) armed conflict' in Andrew Clapham and Paola Gaeta (eds) *The Oxford handbook of international law in armed conflict* (Oxford University Press, 2014) 353.

17 Rome Statute of the International Criminal Court (1998), art 8(2)(f).

18 *The Prosecutor v Ramush Haradinaj, Idriz Balaj and Lahi Brahimaj* International Criminal Tribunal of the Former Yugoslavia, Trial Chamber (IT-04-84-T) (3 April 2008).

19 Additional Protocol II (n 15), art 1(1).

20 *The Prosecutor v Ljube Boškoski and Johan Tarčulovski* International Criminal Tribunal of the Former Yugoslavia, Trial Chamber II (IT-04-82-T) (10 July 2008), paras 199–203; See also Annyssa Bellal 'ICRC commentary of Common Article 3: some questions relating to organized armed groups and the applicability of IHL' *EJIL: Talk!* 5 October 2017.

21 'How is the term "armed conflict" defined in international humanitarian law?' International Committee of the Red Cross (ICRC) Opinion Paper (March 2008) 3 https://www.icrc.org/en/doc/assets/files/other/opinion-paper-armed-conflict .pdf (accessed 5 May 2020).

22 See Rome Statute of the International Criminal Court (n 17), art 28(a).

23 As above, art 28(a)(ii).

24 *The Prosecutor v Jean-Pierre Bemba Gombo* International Criminal Court, Trial Chamber III (ICC-01/05-01/08) (21 March 2016).

25 As above, para 199.

26 As above.

27 As above.

28 As above, para 730.

29 As above, para 731.

30 Rome Statute of the International Criminal Court (n 17), para 8.

31 *The Prosecutor v Jean-Pierre Bemba Gombo* International Criminal Court, The Appeals Chamber (ICC-01/05-01/08) (8 June 2018), para 171.

32 As above, para 191
33 As above, para 193.
34 As above.
35 *The Prosecutor v Jean-Pierre Bemba Gombo* International Criminal Court, The Appeals Chamber (ICC-01/05-01/08) (14 June 2018) (Concurring Separate Opinion of Judge Eboe-Osuji), para 258 https://www.icc-cpi.int/RelatedReco rds/CR2018_03077.PDF (accessed 5 May 2020).
36 Additional Protocol II (n 15), art 1(1).
37 Sivakumaran *The law of non-international armed conflict* (n 16) 186.
38 *The Prosecutor v Jean Paul Akayesu* (n 14), para 626.
39 For more on the armed group, please see Jideofor Adibe *Nigeria without Nigerians? Boko Haram and the crisis in Nigeria's nation-building project* (Adonis & Abbey Publishers Ltd, 2012); Hakeem Onapajo, Ufo O Uzodike and Ayo Whetho 'Boko Haram terrorism in Nigeria: the international dimension' (2012) 19(3) *South African Journal of International Affairs* 337; Daniel E Agbiboa 'Why Boko Haram exists: the relative deprivation perspective' (2013) 3(1) *African Conflict and Peacebuilding Review* 144; Ojochenemi J David, Lucky E Asuelime and Hakeem Onapajo *Boko haram: the socioeconomic drivers* (Springer, 2015); Hussein Solomon *Terrorism and counter-terrorism in Africa: fighting insurgency from Al Shabaab, Ansar Dine and Boko Haram* (Springer, 2015); Andrew Walker '*Eat the heart of the infidel': the harrowing of Nigeria and the rise of Boko Haram* (C Hurst & Co (Publishers) Ltd, 2016); Caroline Varin *Boko Haram and the war on terror* (ABC-CLIO, LLC, 2016); Iro Aghedo 'Old wine in a new bottle: ideological and operational linkages between Maitatsine and Boko Haram revolts in Nigeria' in James J Hentz and Hussein Solomon (eds) *Understanding Boko Haram: terrorism and insurgency in Africa* (Routledge, 2017) 65; Alexander Thurston *Boko Haram: the history of an African jihadist movement* (Princeton University Press, 2018); Brandon Kendhammer and Carmen McCain *Boko Haram* (Ohio University Press, 2018); John Maszka *Al-Shabaab and Boko Haram: guerrilla insurgency or strategic terrorism?* (World Scientific Publishing Europe Ltd, 2018); Godwin O Anyalemechi 'Terrorism and cross-border insurgency as new threats and challenges to peace and security in Africa: the Boko Haram insurgency' in John-Mark Iyi and Hennie Strydom (eds) *Boko Haram and international law* (Springer, 2018) 121; Olumuyiwa T Faluyi et al. *Boko Haram's terrorism and the Nigerian state: federalism, politics and policies* (Springer, 2019); Edlyne E Anugwom *The Boko Haram insurgence in Nigeria: perspectives from within* (Palgrave Macmillan, 2019); Ona Ekhomu *Boko Haram: security considerations and the rise of an insurgency* (CRC Press, 2020); Akali Omeni *Insurgency and war in Nigeria: regional fracture and the fight against Boko Haram* (Bloomsbury Publishing, 2020)
40 Report on Preliminary Examination Activities 2012 (November 2012), para 89.
41 Counter Extremism Project *Boko Haram* (2002); John Nugent 'Boko Haram's leadership crisis' *Forbes* 20 September 2013; Mustapha Kulungu 'Does Boko Haram pose a threat to the US?' (2019) 11(2) *Counter Terrorist Trends and Analyses* https://www.jstor.org/stable/pdf/26627975.pdf?refreqid=excelsior% 3Aaf25f74202b62f361b9d8bb1c77eb83f (accessed 5 May 2020).
42 Jacob Zenn 'Islamic state in West Africa province's factional disputes and the battle with Boko Haram' (2020) 18(6) *Terrorism Monitor* 6 https://jamestown

.org/program/islamic-state-in-west-africa-provinces-factional-disputes-and-the-battle-with-boko-haram/ (accessed 5 May 2020).

43 'Boko haram conflict causing misery to millions 10 years on' *Norwegian Refugee Council* 23 July 2019.

44 Conway Waddington 'In the fight against Boko Haram, the Multinational Joint Task Force limps forward' (2015) 7 *Africa Conflict Monitor* 50; Babatunde F Obamamoye 'Counter-terrorism, Multinational Joint Task Force and the missing components' (2017) 15(4) *African Identities* 428; Usman A Tar and Adejoh Sunday 'Military alliance and counter-terrorism in sub-Saharan Africa: the Multi-national Joint Task Force in perspective' (2017) 5(2) *Covenant University Journal of Politics and International Affairs* 1; Isaac O Albert 'Rethinking the functionality of the Multinational Joint Task Force in managing the Boko Haram crisis in the Lake Chad Basin' (2017) 42(3) *Africa Development* 119; Willibroad Dze-Ngwa 'The Multinational Joint Task Force against Boko Haram: rethinking military interventions' (2018) 6(7) *International Journal of Liberal Arts and Social Science* 15; Camillo Casola 'Multinational Joint Task Force: security cooperation in the Lake Chad Basin' *Italian Institute for International Political Studies (Commentary)* 19 March 2020.

45 'Responding to the needs of people affected by armed conflict in Yobe state, Nigeria' *International Committee of the Red Cross (Article)* 29 July 2019; International Committee of the Red Cross 'Facts & Figures: ICRC in Nigeria' (January–June 2019).

46 'Fighting Boko Haram in Chad: beyond military measures' *International Crisis Group* (Africa Report No 246, 8 March 2017); 'Niger army repels Boko Haram attack, 50 extremists killed – govt' *Africa News* 17 March 2020 https://www.youtube.com/watch?v=TbcpEh_s1xA (accessed 5 May 2020); 'Chadian troops "kill 1,000 Boko Haram fighters" in Lake Chad' *Al Jazeera* 9 April 2020; Daniel Eizenga 'Chad's escalating fight against Boko Haram' *Africa Center for Strategic Studies (Spotlight)* 20 April 2020.

47 See also Emrah Kekilli, Khayri Omar and Ibrahim B Abdoulaye 'Anatomy of a terrorist organization: Boko Haram' (Foundation for Political, Economic and Social Research (SETA), 2018).

48 'Nigeria's Boko Haram "seize" Bama town in Borno' *BBC (News)* 2 September 2014; 'Nigeria says it has ousted Boko Haram from town of Bama' *BBC (News)* 17 March 2015; 'Boko Haram islamists still control parts of northeastern Nigeria' *DW* 19 May 2018; Abdulkareem Haruna 'Special report: increasing Boko Haram attacks on highways threaten to cut Borno state from Nigeria' *Premium Times* 23 January 2020.

49 'Facing the challenge of the Islamic State in West Africa Province' *International Crisis Group* (Africa Report No 273, 16 May 2019); Samantha Raphelson 'Islamic state group in Nigeria reportedly executes Christian hostages' *NPR* 27 December 2019; Bassim Al-Hussaini 'ISWAP, terror group in Nigeria, rebrands, reversing tradition' *Premium Times* 27 February 2020.

50 David J Cantor 'As deadly as armed conflict? Gang violence and forced displacement in the Northern Triangle of Central America' (2016) 23(34) *Agenda Internacional* 77; See generally Elin C Ranum 'Street gangs in Guatemala' in Thomas Bruneau, Lucía Damme and Elizabeth Skinner (eds) *Maras: gang violence and security in Central America* (University of Texas Press, 2011) 71; Sonja Wolf *Mano dura: the politics of gang control in El Salvador* (University of Texas Press, 2017).

51 'Violence in Niger Delta expands into gang war' *CNN* 8 August 2007.

52 'With gangs aplenty, Lagos inner streets know little joy' *The Guardian (Nigeria)* 13 November 2018; 'Nigeria president condemns latest killings in northwestern Sokoto state' *Reuters* 20 July 2019.

53 'Nigeria president condemns latest killings in northwestern Sokoto state' (n 52).

54 'Brutal violence in northern Nigeria forces thousands into Niger' *UN Refugee Agency* 27 September 2019; 'Lawlessness double displaced from NW Nigeria to 40,000 – UNHCR' *Euronews* 27 September 2019.

55 Neil Munshi 'Overwhelmed by bandits, Nigeria state offer amnesty' *Financial Times* 13 October 2019; 'Armed gang kills at least 30 in northwest Nigeria, police say' *Reuters* 15 February 2020; 'Motorcycle gang on the rampage in Nigeria' *Defence Web* 17 February 2020.

56 'At least 50 killed in northern Nigeria "bandit" attacks' *Al Jazeera* 2 March 2020.

57 See Adam Nossiter 'New threat in Nigeria as militants split off' *The New York Times* 23 April 2013; Will Hartley 'Re-emergence of Ansaru in northern Nigeria raises threat of targeted violence against western nationals and companies' *Jane's Terrorism & Insurgency Monitor* 23 January 2020.

58 Olayiwola Abegunrin *Nigerian foreign policy under military rule, 1966–1999* (Greenwood Publishing Group Inc, 2003) 26.

59 Toyin Falola and Julius O Ihonvbere *The rise and fall of Nigeria's Second Republic: 1979–1984* (Zed Books, 1985); Aderemi Ajibewa 'The Third Republic and Nigeria's foreign policy options ' in Bamidele A Ojo (ed) *Third Republic: the problems and prospects of political transition to civil rule* (Nova Science Publishers Inc, 1998); Shola J Omotola 'Explaining electoral violence in Africa's "new" democracies' *Accord* AJCR 2010/3 https://www.accord.org.za/ajcr-issues/explaining-electoral-violence-in-africas-new-democracies/ (accessed 6 May 2020); Isaac O Albert 'Electoral violence in the Nigerian "Fourth Republic": the paradox of democracy' (2011) 3(239) *Afrique Contemporaine* 105; Chinwe Nwanna 'Governance and local government elections in Nigeria's Fourth Republic' in Osita Agbu (ed) *Elections and governance in Nigeria's Fourth Republic* (Council for the Development of Social Science Research in Africa, 2016) 53; Dhikru A Yagboyaju and Adeoye O Akinola 'Nigerian state and the crisis of governance: a critical exposition' (2019) *SAGE Open* https://doi.org/10.1177/2158244019865810 (accessed 6 May 2020).

60 See Kaduna State Government *White Paper on the report of the Committee to investigate causes of riots and disturbances in Kaduna State* 6–12 March 1987; Kaduna State of Nigeria *Report of Zangon Kataf (Market) riots judicial commission of inquiry* (June 1992); Toure Kazah-Toure 'The political economy of ethnic conflicts and governance in southern Kaduna, Nigeria: [de]constructing a contested terrain' (1999) 24(1) *Africa Development* 109; Kaduna State of Nigeria *White Paper on the report of Judicial Commission of Inquiry into Kaduna State religious disturbances of February 2000* (2001); Terhemba N Ambe-Uva 'Identity politics and the Jos crisis: evidence, lessons and challenges of good governance' (2010) 2(3) *African Journal of History and Culture* 42; Jana Krause 'A deadly cycle: ethno-religious conflict in Jos, Plateau state, Nigeria' (Geneva Declaration Secretariat Working Paper, June 2011); Henrik Angerbrandt 'Political decentralisation and conflict: the Sharia crisis in Kaduna, Nigeria' (2011) 29(1) *Journal of Contemporary African Studies* 15; Ignatius A

Kaigama *Peace, not war: a decade of interventions in the Plateau state crises (2001–2011)* (Hamtul Press Ltd, 2012); Henrik Angerbrandt 'Religion, ethnicity and citizenship: demands for territorial self-determination in southern Kaduna, Nigeria' (2014) 33(2) *Journal of Contemporary African Studies* 232; Nigerian Senate *Interim report of the Senate Ad Hoc Committee on Southern Kaduna crisis and other parts of the country* (2017); Kingsley L Madueke 'From neighbours to deadly enemies: excavating landscapes of territoriality and ethnic violence in Jos, Nigeria' (2018) 36(1) *Journal of Contemporary African Studies* 87.

61 Isaac T Sampson 'Religious violence in Nigeria' *Accord* AJCR 2012/1 https://www.accord.org.za/ajcr-issues/religious-violence-in-nigeria/ (accessed 6 May 2020).

62 Universal Declaration of Human Rights, adopted by the UN General Assembly Resolution 217 A (III) of 10 December 1948; International Covenant on Civil and Political Rights, adopted by the UN General Assembly Resolution 2200A (XXI), UN Doc A/6316 (16 December 1966); International Covenant on Economic, Social and Cultural Rights, adopted by the UN General Assembly Resolution 2200A (XXI), UN Doc A/6316 (16 December 1966); African Charter on Human and Peoples' Rights (1981); See generally Susan Marks and Andrew Clapham *International human rights lexicon* (Oxford University Press, 2005); Mark Gibney *International human rights law: returning to universal principles* (Rowman & Littlefield Publishers Inc, 2008); Walter Kälin and Jörg Künzli *The law of international human rights protection* (Oxford University Press, 2009); Daniel J Whelan *Indivisible human rights: a history* (University of Pennsylvania Press, 2010); Olivier de Schutter *International human rights law: cases, materials, commentary* (Cambridge University Press, 2010); Frans Viljoen *International human rights law in Africa* (Oxford University Press, 2012); Ilias Bantekas and Lutz Oette *International human rights law and practice* (Cambridge University Press, 2013); Jack Donnelly *Universal human rights in theory and practice* (Cornell University Press, 2013); Christian Tomuschat *Human rights: between idealism and realism* (Oxford University Press, 2014); Dinah L Shelton *Advanced introduction to international human rights law* (Edward Elgar Publishing Limited, 2014); Dinah Shelton *Remedies in international human rights law* (Oxford University Press, 2015); Manisuli Ssenyonjo *Economic, social and cultural rights in international law* (Hart Publishing, 2016); Rhona KM Smith *International human rights law* (Oxford University Press, 2018); Danwood M Chirwa 'The Universal Declaration of Human Rights, economic, social and cultural rights and human rights discourse' in Carla Ferstman et al. (eds) *Contemporary human rights challenges: the Universal Declaration of Human Rights and its continuing relevance* (Routledge, 2019).

63 Communication 155/96: *Social and Economic Rights Action Center (SERAC) and Center for Economic and Social Rights (CESR) v Nigeria*, para 44–47.

64 Amnesty International *At the mercy of the government: violation of the right to an effective remedy in Badia East, Lagos state, Nigeria* (AFR 44/017/2014).

65 International Law Commission *Draft articles on the protection of persons in the event of disaster* (2016), art 3(a).

66 Orji Sunday 'It rains, it pours, it floods: Nigeria's growing seasonal problem' *African Arguments* 15 November 2018; Okechukwu Nnodim 'NEMA prepares against flooding' *Punch* 30 April 2019.

67 Human Rights Watch *The price of oil: corporate responsibility and human rights violations in Nigeria's oil producing communities* (Human Rights Watch, 1999); Ike Okonta and Oronto Douglas *Where vultures feast: Shell, human rights, and oil in the Niger Delta* (Verso, 2003); Irina Romanova *Oil boom in Nigeria and its consequences for the country's economic development* (GRIN Verlag, 2007); Christian O Opukri and Ibaba S Ibaba 'Oil induced environmental degradation and internal population displacement in the Nigeria's Niger Delta' (2008) 10(1) *Journal of Sustainable Development in Africa* 173; Cyril Obi 'Nigeria's Niger Delta: understanding the complex drivers of violent oil-related conflict' (2009) 34(2) *Africa Development* 103; John Agbonifo 'Oil, insecurity, and subversive patriots in the Niger Delta: the Ogoni as agent of revolutionary change' (2009) 26(2) *Journal of Third World Studies* 71; Jean-Paul Azam 'Betting on displacement: oil, violence, and the switch to civilian rule in Nigeria' Toulouse School of Economics Working Paper Series 09-034 (10 May 2009); Michael Peel *A swamp full of dollars: pipelines and paramilitaries at Nigeria's oil frontier* (Bloomsbury Publishing, 2009); Francis G Umukoro 'Politicisation and underdevelopment of the Niger Delta region' in Victor Ojakorotu (ed) *Anatomy of the Niger Delta crisis: causes, consequences and opportunities for peace* (LIT Verlag, 2010) 47; Isiaka A Badmus 'Oiling the guns and gunning for oil: oil violence, arms proliferation and the destruction of Nigeria's Niger-Delta' (2010) 2(1) *Journal of Alternative Perspectives in the Social Sciences* 323; Rhuks Ako 'The struggle for resource control and violence in the Niger Delta' in Cyril Obi and Siri A Rustad (eds) *Oil and insurgency in the Niger Delta: managing the complex politics of petro-violence* (Zed Books, 2011); Prince C Mmom and Chimezie F Igwe 'Environmental degradation resulting from oil exploitation, and population displacement in the Niger Delta, Nigeria' (2012) 1 *Journal of Environmental Science and Engineering* 125; Omolade Adunbi *Oil wealth and insurgency in Nigeria* (Indiana University Press, 2015); John K Wangbu *The Niger Delta paradox: impoverished in the midst of abundance* (Safari Books Ltd, 2018).

68 This has led to litigation, see generally *Ikpede v The Shell BP Petroleum Development Company Nigeria Limited* (1973) MWSJ 61; *Mon & Anor v Shell Petroleum Development Company Nigeria Limited* (1973) 1 RSLR 71; *Chinda & 5 Others v Shell-BP Petroleum Development Company of Nigeria Limited* (1974) 2 RSLR 1; *Umudje & Anor v Shell-BP Petroleum Development Company of Nigeria Limited* 1975) 9-11 SC 155; *Amos & Ors (for themselves as individual and on behalf of Ogbia Community Brass Division) v Shell B.P Petroleum Development Company of Nigeria Limited and Anor* (1977) 6 SC 109; *Nwadiaro & 2 Others v Shell Petroleum Development Company Nigeria Limited* (1990) 5 NWLR. (Part 150) 322; *Shell Petroleum Development Company of Nigeria Limited v Ambah* (1991) 3 NWLR (Part 593) 1; *Shell Petroleum Development Company of Nigeria Limited v Enoch & 2 Ors* (1992) 8 NWLR (Part 259) 335; *Shell Petroleum Development Company of Nigeria Limited v Uzoaru & 3 Ors* (For themselves and as representing the Umunnaka Ukwu village of Oguta) (1994) 9 NWLR (Part 366) 51; *ELF Nigeria Ltd v Sillo & Anor (For themselves and on behalf of Sillo family of Obodo)* (1994) 6 NWLR (Part 350) 258; *Shell Petroleum Development Company Nigeria Limited v Farah & 7 Others* (1995) 3 NWLR. (Part 382) 148; *Shell Petroleum Development Company Nigeria Limited v Udi* (1996) 6 NWLR (Part 455) 483; *Shell Petroleum Development Company Nigeria Ltd v*

Otoko (1996) 6 NWLR (Part 150) 639; *Ogiale v Shell Petroleum Development Company Nigeria Limited* (1997) 1 NWLR (Pt. 480) 148; *Douglas v Shell Petroleum Development Company Nigeria Limited* (1999) 2 NWLR (Part 591) 466; *Shell Petroleum Development Company Nigeria Ltd v Amaro & Ors* (2000) 10 NWLR (Part 675) 248; *Shell Petroleum Development Company Nigeria Limited v Isaiah* (2001) 11 N.W.L.R. (Part 723) 168; *Shell Petroleum Development Company, Nigeria Ltd v Tiebo VII & Others* (2005) 3-4 S.C; *Shell Petroleum Development Company Nigeria Limited v Edamkue & Others* (2009) 10 SCM 150.

69 Kampala Convention (n 2), art 5(4).

70 Paris Agreement (2015), Preamble.

71 For more on climate change, please see Camille Parmesan and Gary Yohe 'A globally coherent fingerprint of climate change impacts across natural systems' (2003) 421 *Nature* 37; Marcel Leroux *Global warming – myth or reality? the erring ways of climatology* (Springer, 2006); Hans-Martin Füssel and Richard JT Klein 'Climate change vulnerability assessments: an evolution of conceptual thinking' (2006) 75 *Climate Change* 301; Filippo Giorgi and Piero Lionello 'Climate change projections for the Mediterranean region' (2008) 63(2/3) *Global and Planetary Change* 90; Scott R Loarie et al. 'The velocity of climate change' (2009) 462 *Nature* 1052; Barrie A Pittock *Climate change: the science, impacts and solutions* (Earthscan, 2009); Jon Barnett and John Campbell *Climate change and Small Island Small States: power, knowledge and the South Pacific* (Earthscan, 2010); Robert O Keohane and David G Victor 'The regime complex for climate change' (2011) 9(1) *Perspectives on Politics* 7; Michael Reder 'Climate change and human rights' in Ottmar Edenhofer et al. (eds) *Climate change, justice and sustainability: linking climate and development policy* (Springer, 2012) 61; Harriet Bulkeley and Peter Newell *Governing climate change* (Routledge, 2015); Matt McGrath 'Climate change: "Hothouse Earth" risks even if CO2 emissions slashed' *BBC News* 6 August 2018.

72 Intergovernmental Panel on Climate Change *Global warming of 1.5°C* (Intergovernmental Panel on Climate Change, 2019) 51.

73 Ton Dietz 'Ecospace, humanspace and climate change' in Mohamed MA Salih (ed) *Climate change and sustainable development: new challenges for poverty reduction* (Edward Elgar Publishing, 2009) 47; Salisu L Halliru and Da'u A Umar 'Climate change and rural water supply planning in Nigeria' in Walter L Filho (ed) *Climate change and the sustainable use of water resources* (Springer, 2012) 305; Ramasamy Selvaraju 'Implications of climate change for agriculture and food security in the western Asia and northern Africa region' in Mannava VK Sivakumar, Rattan LR Selvaraju and Ibrahim Hamdan (eds) *Climate change and food security in West Asia and North Africa* (Springer, 2013) 27; Sanjay Khajuria 'Water, climate change and sustainable development' in Asit K Biswas and Cecilia Tortajada (eds) *Water security, climate change and sustainable development* (Springer, 2016) 123; Walter L Filho, Isaac K Tetteh and Haruna M Musa 'Trends in climate change in Africa' in Elizabeth Thomas-Hope (eds) *Climate change and food security: Africa and the Caribbean* (Routledge, 2018) 15, 23–24.

74 World Bank *Groundswell: preparing for internal climate migration* (2018).

75 Paris Agreement (n 70).

76 See Kampala Convention (n 2), arts 4(4) & 5(4).

77 Decision 1/CP.16: The Cancun Agreements: Outcome of the work of the Ad Hoc Working Group on Long-term Cooperative Action under the Convention, adopted at the 16th Session of the United Nations Framework Convention on Climate Change Conference of the Parties, Cancun, Mexico (29 November – 10 December 2010); Walter Kälin 'Conceptualising climate-induced displacement' in Jane McAdam (ed) *Climate change and displacement: multidisciplinary perspectives* (Hart Publishing, 2010) 81; Ademola O Jegede 'Indigenous peoples, climate migration and international human rights law in Africa, with reflections on the relevance of the Kampala Convention' in Benoît Mayer and François Crépeau (eds) *Research handbook on climate change, migration and the law* (Edward Elgar, 2017) 169; World Bank *Groundswell: preparing for internal climate migration* (2018); Romola Adeola 'Protecting climate change induced internally displaced persons in Africa: relevance of the Kampala Convention' in Walter Leal Filho (ed) *Handbook of Climate Change Resilience* (Springer, 2019).

78 Huma Haider 'Climate change in Nigeria: impacts and responses' Knowledge, Evidence and Learning for Development (K4D) Helpdesk Report (10 October 2019).

79 Emmanuel Oladipo 'Towards enhancing the adaptive capacity in Nigeria: a review of the country's state of preparedness for climate change adaptation' Henrich Böll Foundation Nigeria (September 2010) 7 https://ng.boell.org/site s/default/files/uploads/2013/10/nigeria_prof_oladipo_final_cga_study.pdf (6 May 2020)

80 Temitope A Ogunrinde et al. 'Analysis of recent changes in rainfall and drought indices in Nigeria, 1981–2015' (2019) 64(14) *Hydrological Sciences Journal* 1755.

81 Sara Vigil 'Green grabbing-induced displacement' (Istituto per gli Studi di Politica Internazionale (ISPI) Commentary, 23 March 2018).

82 Akanimo Sampson 'Don't sell forests, groups urge Nigerian govts' *Scoop (World)* 27 August 2010 https://www.scoop.co.nz/stories/WO1008/S00467 /dont-sell-forests-groups-urge-nigerian-govts.htm (accessed 6 May 2020); Damilola S Olawuyi *The human rights-based approach to carbon finance* (Cambridge University Press, 2016) 88.

83 Huma Haider 'Climate change in Nigeria: impacts and responses' (n 78) 13.

84 International Crisis Group *Herders against farmers: Nigeria's expanding deadly conflict* (Africa Report No 252, 19 September 2017).

85 Amnesty International *Harvest of death: three years of bloody clashes between farmers and herders in Nigeria* (AFR/9503/2018).

86 International Committee of the Red Cross facts and figures: Nigeria in perspective: meeting evolving humanitarian needs (2017).

87 Raphael A Olawepo 'Resettlement and agricultural change in a rural Nigerian environment: the Jebba scheme example' (2006) 2(1) *International Journal of Rural Management* 57; Gebre Yntiso 'Urban development and displacement in Addis Ababa: the impact of resettlement projects on low income households' (2008) 24(2) *Eastern Africa Social Science Research Review* 53; Leben Moro 'Oil development induced displacement in the Sudan' Sir William Luce Fellowship Paper No 10, University of Durham, United Kingdom (2009); Bogumil Terminski 'Oil-induced displacement and resettlement: social problem and human rights issue' Research Paper, School for International Studies, Simon Fraser University, Vancouver (2012); Emeka D Oruonye 'An

assessment of the socio-economic impact of urban development-induced reset-tlement scheme in Nigerian cities: a case study of the Nyamusala – ATC road construction in Jalingo Metropolis, Taraba state' (2012) 3(1) *International Review of Social Sciences and Humanities* 1; John L Oyefara and Bamidele O Alabi 'Socio-economic consequences of development-induced internal displacement and the coping strategies of female victims in Lagos, Nigeria: an ethno-demographic study' (2016) 30(2) *African Population Studies* 2520; Paul O Adekola, Dominic Azuh, Adebanke Olawole-Isaac and Emmanuel Amoo 'Health implication of development-induced internal displacements in Ogun state, Southwestern Nigeria' Proceedings of SOCIOINT 2017 – 4th International Conference on Education, Social Sciences and Humanities, Dubai, United Arab Emirates (10–12 July 2017); Julian H Walker, Barbara Lipietz, Victoria Ohaeri, Victor Onyebueke and Oliver Ujah 'Displacement and the public interest in Nigeria: contesting developmental rationales for displace-ment' (2019) *Development in Practice* 1; Caroline Aboda, Frank Mugagga, Patrick Byakagaba and Goretti Nabanoga 'Development induced displace-ment: a review of risks faced by communities in developing countries' (2019) 7(2) *Sociology and Anthropology* 100.

88 See Romola Adeola *Development-induced displacement and human rights in Africa: the Kampala Convention* (Routledge, 2021).

89 Günther Baechler *Violence through environmental discrimination: causes, Rwanda arena, and conflict model* (Kluwer Academic Publishers, 1999) 191.

90 Romola Adeola 'The legal protection of development-induced displaced per-sons in Africa' (2017) 10(1) *African Journal of Legal Studies* 91.

91 Tina Wallace 'Agricultural projects and land in northern Nigeria' (1980) 17 *Review of African Political Economy* 59, 61; PR Maurya 'Farmer partici-pation in irrigation development and management' Proceedings of a National Workshop held at the Institute for Agricultural Research, Samaru, Zaria, Nigeria (7–8 May 1990) 65.

92 Ken Swindell *Farm labour* (Cambridge University Press, 1985) 167; Tom Forrest *Politics and economic development in Nigeria: updated edited* (Avalon Publishing, 1995) 193.

93 William M Adams *Wasting the rain: rivers, people and planning in Africa* (Earthscan, 1992) 119–120.

94 Minority Rights Group International *State of the World's minorities 2006 – Nigeria* (22 December 2005) https://www.refworld.org/docid/48abdd6fc.html (accessed 6 May 2020); Julia Maxted 'Exploitation of energy resources in Africa' in Scott R Sernau (ed) *Contemporary readings in globalization* (Sage Publications Inc, 2008) 163, 166.

95 Tume Ahemba 'Nigeria evicted 800,000 Abuja residents: report' *Reuters* 15 May 2008; Amnesty International *"Just move them": forced evictions in Port Harcourt, Nigeria* (2010); Elijah BA Agbaje 'Modernisation, urban renewal and the social cost of development' (2013) 4(10) *Mediterranean Journal of Social Sciences* 318, 321; Bons N Obiadi et al. 'Where is home for the Abuja, Nigeria urban poor' (2019) 8(1) *Mgbakoigba, Journal of African Studies* 50.

96 Centre on Housing Rights and Eviction and Social and Economic Rights Action Center *The myth of the Abuja master plan: Nigeria* (Mission Report, May 2008).

97 Spaces for Change *Demolishing foundations of peace* (2012) 18.

98 Internal Displacement Monitoring Centre & Norwegian Refugee Council *Nigeria: multiple displacement crisis overshadowed by Boko Haram* (2014).

99 'Over 30,000 homeless after police use demolition by fire and bulldozer working in dead of night destroy Otodo Gbame community despite subsisting injunction' *Justice & Empowerment Initiative – Nigeria* (Press Release, 10 November 2016) https://static1.squarespace.com/static/535d0435e4b0586b 1fc64b54/t/582412f56a49630e4fdb3b06/1478759158239/Otodo+Gbame+Pre ss+Release+%28Nov+10+2016%29.pdf (accessed 6 May 2020).

100 Chris Arsenault 'Nigerian farmers face eviction by foreign mega-plantation – TRFN' *Reuters* 28 January 2015.

101 Center for Environmental Education and Development, Environmental Rights Action, GRAIN and Global Justice Now 'Dominion farms' land grab in Nigeria: farmers in Taraba state refuse to give up their lands for massive rice plantation project backed by the G8' (January 2015).

102 As above, 4.

103 See Kampala Convention (n 2) art 4(4)(e).

104 Protocol to the African Charter on Human and Peoples' Rights on the Rights of Women in Africa (2003), art 1(g).

105 Girls Not Brides *Nigeria – child marriage around the world* https://www.gir lsnotbrides.org/child-marriage/nigeria/ (accessed 6 May 2020).

106 Stephanie Sinclair 'Child, bride, mother: Nigeria' *New York Times* 27 January 2017.

107 As above; 'Resistance continues to ending child marriage in northern Nigeria' *VOA* 22 March 2018 https://www.youtube.com/watch?v=VI_U3tlkWd8 (accessed 6 May 2020).

3 Applicable frameworks on internally displaced persons in Nigeria

3.1 Introduction

Having examined the definition and causes of internal displacement, this chapter examines the normative framework on internally displaced persons (IDPs) in Nigeria. In framing the response to internal displacement, it is imperative to consider the legal landscape for the protection and assistance of IDPs. In doing so, it is crucial to understand what exists and how protection can be advanced. In considering the legal regime on IDPs in Nigeria, this chapter is divided into three parts. The first part examines the Constitution, which is the primary source of law in Nigeria. In the first chapter, it was stated that the Constitution 'includes a bill of rights in Chapter IV, mostly comprising of civil and political rights, and has a set of directive principles of state policy, however, these are non-justiciable'.[1] It is crucial to understand the extent to which the Constitution incorporates relevant protection for IDPs. Following the discussion, this chapter examines the general frameworks related to the protection of IDPs and afterwards considers the Kampala Convention as a supplementary law.

3.2 The 1999 Nigerian Constitution

The apex of legal protection is the 1999 Nigerian Constitution (Constitution), specifically, the provision of Chapter IV which incorporates Fundamental Human Rights.[2]

Section 33(1) of the Constitution provides for the right to life and prohibits unlawful deprivation of life. Being fundamental to the realisation of other rights, the right to life is imperative to the protection of IDPs significantly, also in the context of conflict situations. In *Mustapha v Governor of Lagos State & Ors*, the Supreme Court emphasised that the 'right to life is common to all human beings. It is a human right attaching to man as man because of his humanity'.[3] In the context of internal displacement, principle

DOI: 10.4324/9781003146025-3

10 of the United Nations (UN) Guiding Principles on Internal Displacement (Guiding Principles) further emphasises the need for IDPs to be protected against specific breaches as with threats and incitements of these breaches, specifically, '(a) genocide; (b) murder; (c) summary or arbitrary executions; and (d) enforced disappearances, including abduction or unacknowledged detention, threatening or resulting in death'.[4] Moreover, this right further requires the protection of IDPs (who are not taking part in hostilities) from 'attacks or other acts of violence'.[5] For IDPs, notably in the conflict context, such as with the Boko Haram situation, the protection of this right requires that specific measures are adopted to safeguard against deprivation both from state and non-state actors. In principle, adequate conflict early warning systems will be integral to this process.

Section 34 of the Constitution relates to respect for dignity of the person. Specifically, it prohibits 'torture', 'inhuman or degrading treatment', and emphasises that 'no person shall be held in slavery or servitude' and 'no person shall be required to perform forced or compulsory labour'.[6] In *Rhodes & Anor v IGP & Ors*, the Court of Appeal, per Ikyegh JCA, expressed that[7]

[w]hat degrades or devalues a person's exalted estimation of his societal status or standing amounts to an assault on the dignity of that person. But before the conclusion that such person's dignity has been eroded is reached it must be shown that the act complained of falls within the context of section 34(1) of the 1999 Constitution, as amended, indicating the act complained of subjected the person to torture or to inhuman or degrading treatment or the person was held in slavery or servitude or the person was required to perform forced labour or compulsory labour.

The Guiding Principles prohibits displacement that violates the 'rights to life, dignity, liberty and security of those affected',[8] and further reinforces the right of everyone to dignity.[9] In the context of development-induced displacement (DID), for instance, practical measures towards protecting the right to dignity will include avoiding displacement in unfavourable weather conditions, ensuring that displacement does not occur without adequate compensation and resettlement.

Section 35 of the Constitution emphasises the right to personal liberty. In *Aqua v Archibong & Ors*, the Court of Appeal, per Garba JCA, observed that '[a]s a foundation, every citizen of Nigeria has a constitutionally guaranteed right to his personal liberty which cannot be interfered with or violated except as may be permitted by the constitution itself or a law made pursuant thereto'.[10] The Guiding Principles emphasises the right of everyone to 'liberty and security of persons' and prohibits 'arbitrary arrest or detention'.[11] In reinforcing this right in the context of internal displacement, the Guiding Principles accentuates that IDPs 'shall not be interned in or confined to a camp ... [unless] such internment or confinement is absolutely necessary'.[12] The Guiding Principles further emphasises that such 'shall not last longer than required by the circumstances'.[13] Principle 12(3) of the Guiding Principles protects IDPs 'from discriminatory arrest and detention as a result of their displacement' and prohibits taking IDPs 'hostage'.[14]

Section 36 of the Constitution enshrines the right to fair hearing and provides that 'a person shall be entitled to a fair hearing within a reasonable time by a court or other tribunal established by law and constituted in such manner as to secure its independence and impartiality'.[15] In *T.M. Orugbo & Anor v Bulara Una & Ors*, the Supreme Court, per Tobi JSC, emphasised that the 'fair hearing principle entrenched in the Constitution is so fundamental in the judicial process or the administration of justice that breach of it will vitiate or nullify the whole proceedings'.[16] In addition to civil and criminal proceedings, generally securing this right is important for IDPs particularly in situations of property, housing and land rights. The African Union Convention for the Protection and Assistance of Internally Displaced Persons in Africa (Kampala Convention), in article 11(4), require states to 'establish appropriate mechanisms providing for simplified procedures where necessary, for resolving disputes relating to the property of internally displaced persons'.[17] Protecting the right to fair hearing in this context will require a competent, independent and impartial judiciary, equality of access for various categories of persons including women, the elderly and persons with disabilities (PWDs) and access to legal aid.

Section 37 of the Constitution safeguards the right to privacy. Related to 'personal autonomy',[18] the right to privacy is integral to the realisation of other rights given the fact that it facilitates the enjoyment of other fundamental rights and reinforces the pertinence of non-interference. Specifically, article 37 of the Constitution protects the right to privacy for 'citizens, their homes, correspondence, telephone conversations and telegraphic communications'.[19] In *Nwali v Ebsiec & Ors*, the Court of Appeal, per Agim JCA, elaborated on the nature of this right emphasising that textually, there are five dimensions of this right and that the meaning of 'privacy of citizens' while 'not directly obvious on its face ... is obviously very wide as it does not define the specific aspects of the privacy of citizen it protects'.[20] The Court of Appeal, per Agim, interpreted privacy of citizens 'generally, liberally and expansively to include privacy of citizens' body, life, person, thought, belief, conscience, feelings, views, decisions (including ... plans and choices), desires, health, relationships, character, material possessions, family life, activities et cetera'.[21] For IDPs, the protection of this right is fundamental to the realisation of other pertinent rights, given the fact that it reinforces the need to prohibit arbitrary interference into personal spaces.

Protecting IDPs' right to privacy will require, for instance, the establishment of specific measures geared towards ensuring adequate housing, independent living, security and safety.

Section 38 of the Constitution accentuates the right to freedom of thought, conscience and religion 'including freedom to change ... religion or belief, and freedom (either alone or in community with others, and in public or in private)'.[22] In *Medical and Dental Practitioners Disciplinary Tribunal v Okonkwo*, the Supreme Court, per Ayoola JSC, emphasised that[23]

> The right to freedom of thought, conscience or religion implies a right not to be prevented, without lawful justification, from choosing the course of one's life, fashioned on what one believes in, and a right not to be coerced into acting contrary to religious belief. The limits of these freedoms, as in all cases, are where they impinge on the rights of others or where they put the welfare of society or public health in jeopardy. The sum total of the rights of privacy and of freedom of thought, conscience or religion which an individual has, put in a nutshell, is that an individual should be left alone to choose a course for his life, unless a clear and compelling overriding state interest justifies the contrary. The law's role is to ensure the fullness or liberty when there is no danger to public interest. Ensuring liberty of conscience and freedom of religion is an important component of that fullness.

Protecting the right to freedom of thought, conscience and religion for IDPs will require setting measures in place that prohibits discrimination whether in camps or host communities. Principle 22(1) of the Guiding Principles reinforces this right emphasising the need to ensure that whether in camps or outside camps, IDPs are protected from discrimination in the enjoyment of their rights including the 'right to freedom of thought, conscience, religion or belief, opinion and expression'.[24]

Section 39 of the Constitution emphasises the freedom of expression. In *Aviomoh v COP & Anor*, the Court of Appeal, per Yahaya JCA, emphasised that[25]

> It is correct that the freedom of expression and freedom to hold opinions, are rights accruing to Nigerian Citizens. Section 39(1) of the 1999 Constitution as amended provides: – 'Every person shall be entitled to freedom of expression, including freedom to hold opinions and to receive and impart ideas and information without interference.'

This right is imperative to the furtherance of democratic societies as it guarantees the ability of all persons to communicate freely and express their opinions. The right to freedom of expression is integral to participation in the socio-political life of societies. And for IDPs, the right to freedom of expression is essential to the furtherance of political participation, involvement in public affairs, humanitarian assistance and the realisation of durable solutions.

Section 40 of the Constitution incorporates the right to assembly. Specifically, it provides that 'every person shall be entitled to assemble freely and associate with other persons, and in particular he may form or belong to any political party, trade union or any other association for the protection of his interests'.[26] In *Okafor & Ors v Ntoka & Ors*, the Court of Appeal, per Ogunwumiju JCA, expressed that '[t]he right to peaceful assembly and association entitles every person to associate freely with others'.[27] The Guiding Principles reinforces the rights of IDPs to 'associate freely and participate equally in community affairs'.[28]

Section 41 of the Constitution contains the right to free movement and residence. In *Okafor v Lagos State Govt and Anor*, the Court of Appeal, per Georgewill JCA, emphasised that[29]

> The Nigerian Constitution in cognizance of the inalienable right of the citizen, notwithstanding his station or standing in life, to freedom of movement to breath the fresh air and walk the great lands of this Country, Nigeria, free from the Tsunamis and Hurricanes of other far distant Countries, has provided for the freedom of movement as a Constitutionally guaranteed right of the citizens by virtue of Section 41(1) of the Constitution of Nigeria 1999 (as amended).

Integral to the realisation of human development, the right to free movement and residence provides IDPs with the opportunity to seize on livelihood capacities in and outside camps.[30] Moreover, the right to freedom and movement reinforces the need to ensure that measures are set in place to avoid arbitrary displacement given the fact that the forcible or involuntary nature of internal displacement is contrary to the ideation of liberty or freedom of movement and residence.[31]

Section 42 of the Constitution reinforces non-discrimination. In *Lafia Local Govt v Executive Govt, Nasarawa State & Ors*,[32] the Supreme Court, per Rhodes-Vivour JSC, reinforced the fact that:

> Section 42 of the Constitution guarantees to every citizen of Nigeria freedom from discrimination on the basis of belonging to a particular community, ethnic group, place of origin, sex, religion or political opinion. The discrimination complained about must emanate from a law in force in Nigeria, or any executive or administrative action of the Government.

Given that displacement may arise from discriminatory practices that reinforce marginalisation, protecting the right to non-discrimination is important in preventing and responding to situations of internal displacement. As an assertation of equality, non-discrimination is a pertinent cornerstone of international human rights law countering unjustifiable disparate treatment. Moreover, protecting the right to non-discrimination is imperative in ensuring that specific categories of persons whose vulnerabilities may be exacerbated by situations of internal displacement are protected, in particular: women, children, persons with disabilities.

Section 43 of the Constitution protects the right to property while section 44 explicitly sets out the condition upon which expropriation may occur. In *Kandix Ltd & Anor v AG & Commissioner for Justice, Cross River State & Anor*, the Court of Appeal, per Aka'ahs JCA, emphasised that the 'right to own property is a fundamental right enshrined in the Constitution'.[33] Given that displacement creates situations of dispossession, the protection of the right to property is imperative in ensuring that IDPs are not subjected to arbitrary deprivation of property and/or rendered homeless.

3.3 Relevant Legal frameworks

This section examines normative frameworks that are relevant to internal displacement, and which provide a basis for protecting IDPs.

3.3.1 Human rights

Enacted in 1990, the African Charter on Human and Peoples' Rights (Ratification and Enforcement) Act (ACHPR Act) is the primary human rights legislation in Nigeria. Essentially, it domesticates the African Charter on Human and Peoples' Rights (African Charter) adopted by African Heads of State and Government in 1981. The African Charter provides for civil, political, socio-economic and solidarity rights. As the primary framework on human rights in Africa, it has become a significant text from which other normative instruments draw strength. The domestication of the African Charter as national legislation makes the entirety of its provision part of Nigerian law.

In *Abacha v Fawehinmi*, the Supreme Court, per Ogundare JSC, emphasised that having been incorporated nationally, the ACHPR Act 'is now part of the laws of Nigeria and like all other laws the Courts must uphold it'.[34] Evidently, this presupposes the applicability of the provisions of the African Charter, although the extent to which socio-economic rights provided under the African Charter are justiciable is an issue which has garnered significant attention given the fact that such provisions are generally contained in Chapter II of the Constitution as 'Fundamental Objectives and Directive Principles of State Policy' and non-justiciable by virtue of section 6(6)(c) of the Constitution. In *Okogie v Attorney-General of Lagos State*, the Court of Appeal emphasised that 'the arbiter for any breach of and the guardian of the Fundamental Objectives and the Directive Principles of State policy ... is the legislature itself or the electorate'.[35] However, there is an emerging shift in the interpretation of non-justiciability based on section 6(6)(c) of the Constitution. For instance, in *Centre for Oil Pollution Watch v Nigeria National Petroleum Corporation*, the Supreme Court held that 'the non-justiciability of section 6(6)(c) of the Constitution is neither total nor sacrosanct as the subsection provides a leeway by the use of the words "except as otherwise provided by this constitution"'.[36]

By implication, where there are constitutional provisions that give expression to the justiciability of the rights, then such provision will prevail. The Supreme Court made reference, in this case, to section 20 of the Constitution which relates to the protection of the environment providing that 'the state shall protect and improve the environment and safeguard the water, air and land, forest and wildlife of the country'.[37] It was observed by one of the learned counsels in the case that although the provisions of Chapter II of the Constitution are 'ordinarily non-justiciable',[38] there appears to be a 'shift in the thinking of the courts which make the provisions of chapter II of the constitution in certain circumstances justiciable particularly where other provisions of the constitution or other statutes provide for matters contemplated therein'.[39]

Aside from environmental issues where much of this is evident with cases instituted on the premise of environmental legislations, this shift resonates in how the courts also relate to socio-economic rights in the African Charter.[40] For instance, in *Mrs Georgina Ahamefule v Imperial Medical Centre & Dr Alex K Molokwu*, the High Court of Lagos State, per Idowu J, held that the denial of medical care to the applicant based on 'her HIV positive status constitutes a flagrant violation of the right to health guaranteed under article 16 of the African Charter'.[41] Also, in the case of *Odafe & Another v Attorney-General & Others*, the Federal High Court upheld the rights of the applicants (who were in custody) to medical treatment in line with the Prisons Act, the Prisons Regulation Law and the UN Standard Minimum Rules for Treatment of Prisoners. The Federal High Court, per Nwodo J, observed that[42]

> The [African] Charter entrenched the socio-economic rights of a person. The Court is enjoined to ensure the observation of these rights. A dispute concerning socio-economic rights such as the right to medical attention requires the Court to evaluate state policy and give judgment

consistent with the Constitution. I therefore appreciate the fact that the economic cost of embarking on medical provision is quite high. However, the statutes have to be complied with and the state has a responsibility to all the inmates in prison, regardless of the offence involved, as in the instant case where the state has wronged the applicants by not arraigning them for trial before a competent court within a reasonable time and they have been in custody for not less than two years suffering from an illness. They cannot help themselves even if they wanted to because they are detained and cannot consult their doctor.

The African Charter provides an expansive glossary of rights from which to draw on in the furtherance of IDP protection. Evidently, its provisions and the fact that there exists interpretative guidance from the African Commission on Human and Peoples' Rights (African Commission) makes it useful in this process. There is an emerging use of its provisions at the domestic level, specifically in the context of internal displacement. For instance, in *Agemo & Others v Attorney General of Lagos State & Ors*, the High Court of Lagos State, per Onigbanjo J, recognised that the forced evictions or threat of it was 'inhuman, cruel and degrading'.[43] This is evidently in line with provisions of the Constitution and the ACHPR Act.

Another relevant human rights legislation is the Child Rights Act (CRA) which was adopted in 2003. The CRA domesticates the UN Convention on the Rights of the Child and the African Charter on the Rights and Welfare of the Child.[44] Section 171 of the CRA mandate states to safeguard children in need including internally displaced children.[45] The inclusion of protection for internally displaced children is significant given the reality of displacement across the country and its evident impact on children. In light of this provision, the state is required to

(a) safeguard and promote the welfare of the child in need within that State; (b) so far as is consistent with that duty, promote the upbringing of those children by their families, by providing a range and level of services appropriate to the needs of the children.[46]

The CRA is arguably the only domestic legislation that specifically incorporates protection for internally displaced persons, specifically children. However, it is not applicable throughout the 36 states of the federation given that the subject-matter of coverage is a residual issue for which the National Assembly (at the federal level) does not have exclusive jurisdiction. As of 2020, 11 states of the federation were yet to domesticate the CRA.[47] However, it is pertinent to emphasise that the recognition of protection for internally displaced children reflects one of the value additions of the African Charter on the Rights and Welfare of the Child.[48]

There is also a Discrimination against Persons with Disabilities (Prohibition) Act of 2018 which significantly reflects protection for persons with disabilities in Nigeria.[49] Although it does not explicitly mention internal displacement, it provides a significant basis for the furtherance of protection for internally displaced PWDs, particularly in the realisation of their socio-economic rights in order to ensure equality and prevent exclusion and vulnerabilities which situations of internal displacement creates. In 2015, a Violence against Persons (Prohibition) Act (VAP Act) was adopted to 'eliminate violence in private and public life, prohibit all forms of violence against persons and to provide maximum protection and effective remedies for victims and punishment of offenders; and for related matters'.[50] Besides the fact that the legislation protects against abuses such as sexual and gender-based violence, the VAP Act is also significant in its prohibition of harmful traditional practices which is relevant to the prevention of internal displacement occasioned by such practices. But as with the CRA, states of the federation need to incorporate the instrument into their sub-national legislations for application.[51]

3.3.2 Humanitarian law

The Geneva Convention Act of 1960 incorporates the Four Geneva Conventions as part of Nigerian law.[52] In situations of non-international armed conflict, Common Article 3 of the Four Geneva Convention is applicable. While the Four Geneva Conventions have been universally ratified, the Additional Protocols, adopted in 1977, are yet to attain universal ratification. Additional Protocol II specifically relates to non-international armed conflicts. It prohibits the forced displacement of civilian populations except for military necessity or the protection of the civilian population. However, it requires that in case 'such displacements have to be carried out, all possible measures shall be taken in order that the civilian population may be received under satisfactory conditions of shelter, hygiene, health, safety and nutrition'.[53] Nigeria has ratified the Additional Protocols, although the country is yet to domesticate the instrument. However, Additional Protocol II is generally recognised as an effective complement to Common Article 3 of the four Geneva Conventions, incorporated through the Geneva Convention Act.[54] Common Article 3 provides that[55]

> In the case of armed conflict not of an international character occurring in the territory of one of the High Contracting Parties, each Party to the conflict shall be bound to apply, as a minimum, the following provisions:

1. Persons taking no active part in the hostilities, including members of armed forces who have laid down their arms and those placed *hors de combat* by sickness, wounds, detention, or any other cause, shall in all circumstances be treated humanely, without any adverse distinction founded on race, colour, religion or faith, sex, birth or wealth, or any other similar criteria.

   To this end, the following acts are and shall remain prohibited at any time and in any place whatsoever with respect to the above-mentioned persons:

   a) violence to life and person, in particular murder of all kinds, mutilation, cruel treatment and torture;
   b) taking of hostages;
   c) outrages upon personal dignity, in particular humiliating and degrading treatment;
   d) the passing of sentences and the carrying out of executions without previous judgment pronounced by a regularly constituted court, affording all the judicial guarantees which are recognized as indispensable by civilized peoples.

2. The wounded and sick shall be collected and cared for.

3.3.3 Migration law

While Nigeria's Immigration Act regulates international migration, the protection of migrants from a rights-based perspective is not explicit in the document. Arguably, this is due to the fact that the Act was developed in the 1960s in a period when immigration control was mostly a matter of security and there was less focus on rights as emphasised in nascent discussions on migration governance and globally reinforced through the Global Compact on Safe, Orderly and Regular Migration.[56] However, the National Migration Policy which was adopted in 2015 responds to the imperative for protection and emphasises the rights of migrants.[57] In the context of internal displacement, this framework is relevant to the provision of adequate safeguards in order to prevent situations that may result in the displacement of migrants. In some parts of the continent, there have been occasions of generalised violence on the basis of xenophobia in some parts of the continent.[58]

3.3.4 Environmental law

Laws on environmental governance may also be relevant to IDP protection, specifically in situations where displacement is occasioned by natural disasters or environmental degradation. Broadly, these laws include the Land Use Act; Petroleum Act; Oil Pipelines Act; Environmental Impact Assessment Act (EIA Act) and National Environmental Standards and Regulations Enforcement Act (NSREA Act).[59] Specifically within the context of environmental degradation, for instance, section 27(1) of the NSREA Act prohibits the 'discharge in such harmful quantities of any hazardous substance into the air or upon the land and the waters of Nigeria or at the adjoining shorelines'.[60] Prior to the implementation of projects, the EIA Act requires carrying out an assessment of the environment and provides that the 'public or private sector of the economy shall not undertake or embark on public or authorise projects or activities without prior consideration, at an early stage, of their environmental effects'.[61] This provision is particularly relevant in the prevention of development-induced displacement. The Oil Pipelines Act imposes liability on the holder of an oil license where the exercise of the rights granted under the license causes physical or economic damage to a person.[62]

3.3.5 Disaster Law

The law on disaster management is also relevant in the context of internal displacement, notably in the context of displacement induced by disasters. Disaster management is primarily governed by the National Emergency Management Agency (Establishment, Etc) Act of 1999. The National Emergency Management Agency (NEMA) is saddled with the responsibility of disaster management and response. Under the Act establishing NEMA, '"natural or other disasters" includes any disaster arising from any crisis, epidemic, drought, flood, earthquake, storm, train, roads, aircraft, oil spillage or other accidents and mass deportation or repatriation of Nigerians from any other country.'[63] Within the states of federation, there are also State Emergency Management Agencies (SEMAs) that work towards disaster management and response. While the existence of these structures at federal and state levels is significant, a pertinent challenge relates to effective coordination. For instance, during the presentation of NEMA's 2021 budget, for instance, the Senate Committee on Special Duties queried the agency on the point of synergy with other institutions involved in emergency management. In response, the Director-General of NEMA observed that 'the agency sometimes "gets carried away" and does all the work without the sister-agencies.'[64] This is also a challenge in terms of the relationship with SEMA. According to Iroanusi, the Director-General observed that 'the staff of SEMA are sometimes sidelined because of lack of skill and experience.'[65]

3.3.6 Refugee law

Although a different regime of law, refugee law is relevant to the protection of the right of IDPs to seek and enjoy asylum.[66] Implicit in this right is the need for countries of origin and asylum to ensure that IDPs are not prevented from seeking protection. Refugee law is also relevant in situations where refugees return to their countries of origin. As situations of secondary displacement may arise where adequate safeguards are not in place to guarantee safe return, it is imperative for states to ensure that measures are put in place to prevent displacement. The global and regional regime on refugee law[67] is domesticated in Nigeria through the National Commission for Refugees (Establishment, Etc) Act of 2004 (the NCRF Act). Article 5 of the OAU Refugee Convention (incorporated by the NCRF Act) requires that the 'country of origin, on receiving back refugees, shall facilitate their resettlement and grant them the full rights and privileges of nationals of the country, and subject them to the same obligations'.[68] Prior to the adoption of the National Policy on Internally Displaced Persons in 2021 (the Policy), the institutional arrangement for IDPs was significantly located within the National Commission for Refugees (known as the National Commission for Refugees, Migrants and IDPs (NCFRMI). While the NCFRMI was normatively established in order to address refugee concerns, a presidential fiat on the issue of internal displacement included IDP protection in its mandate.[69]

Prior to the establishment of the Ministry of Humanitarian Affairs, Disaster Management and Social Development (FMHADMSD) in 2019, the institutional mandate over IDP protection had been fairly between the NCFRMI and the National Emergency Management Act (NEMA). However, from the legislations establishing these institutions, it is evident that neither institution is specifically saddled with IDP issues. Clearly, the formation of these institutions are specific to issues which, though relevant to IDPs, are not entirely on these populations. For instance, NEMA was established to address situations of disaster, as such, its activities are tailored towards emergency support in disaster situations. However, from the early stages of displacement occasioned by the Boko Haram insurgency, NEMA has been one of most visible institutions in the provision of humanitarian support to IDPs, specifically in providing food and non-food items while also engaging in camp management.[70] Moreover, the NCFRMI was normatively established in order to address refugee concerns. Only through a presidential fiat was the issue of internal displacement included in its mandate.[71] But pragmatically, the NCFRMI positions itself within the context of durable solutions, although visible interventions by the commission often demonstrate an overlap with the activities of NEMA. However, the institutional challenge is a pertinent issue which the Policy addresses reinforcing the lead role of the FMHADMSD in the furtherance of protection and assistance to IDPs.

3.3.7 Land law

Article 44(1) of the Constitution provides that[72]

> No moveable property or any interest in an immovable property shall be taken possession of compulsorily and no right over or interest in any such property shall be acquired compulsorily in any part of Nigeria except in the manner and for the purposes prescribed by a law that, among other things –
>
> (a) requires the prompt payment of compensation therefore and
> (b) gives to any person claiming such compensation a right of access for the determination of his interest in the property and the amount of compensation to a court of law or tribunal or body having jurisdiction in that part of Nigeria.

With respect to land administration, the Land Use Act of 1978 (LUA) is the primary legislation, vesting all lands in the governors of states of the federation and providing that 'such land shall be held in trust and administered for the use and common benefit of all Nigerians'.[73] While this law vests state governors with the competence to grant rights of occupancy, the law further allows the governor of the state to revoke such occupancy.[74] As with the Constitution, LUA is explicit on compensation where a right of occupancy is revoked.[75] Also, under the Mining and Minerals Act, the mining lessee is required to 'pay to the Government the amount of the compensation paid by the Governor to the holder of the certificate of occupancy or the State lessee by reason of the revocation or resumption of possession, as the case maybe',[76] where the right of occupancy is to be revoked.

In *C.S.S Bookshop Ltd v Registered Trustees of Muslim Community in River States & Ors*, the Supreme Court, per Tobi JSC, emphasised that[77]

> Any provision of the law which gives or governs compulsory acquisition of a person's property must be construed by the court fortissimo contra preferentes. Such a statute should be construed by the court strictly against the acquiring authority and sympathetically in favour of the complainant or the owner or possessor of the property against any irregularity in the procedure for acquisition as laid down by the enabling statute.

Article 28(1) of the LUA allows revocation of the right of occupancy 'for overriding public interest'.[78] Notice of such revocation must indicate the ground of revocation, i.e., the overriding public purpose.[79] In *Aso Tim Doz Investment Company Limited v Abuja Markets Management Limited & Anor*, the Nigerian Court of Appeal reinforced the statutory definition of public interest. According to the Court of Appeal, per Mustapha JCA,[80]

> Section 2(b) of the Land Use Act ... defines public interest for which land which was otherwise allocated to an individual could be revoked as: "the requirement of the land by the government of the State or by local government of the State or by local government in the State, in either case public purposes within the State or the requirement of the land by government of the federation for public purpose..."

Article 51 of LUA enumerates the constituent public purpose grounds.[81] In *Ambo Wuyah v Jama'a Local Government, Kafanchan*, the Court of Appeal, per Ogbuinya JCA, was emphatic on the fact that the law does not permit the state to 'acquire, compulsorily or otherwise, any land that belongs to a person and alienate or transfer it to another private individual or body for his/its private use'.[82] In *Goldmark Nigeria Limited & Ors v Ibafon Company Limited & Ors*, the Supreme Court, per Adekeye JSC, emphasised that the public purpose 'test is whether or not the purpose is meant to benefit the public and not just to aid the commercial transaction of a company or a group of people for their own selfish or financial purposes'.[83]

However, what the law regards as public purpose is quite far-reaching and raises questions on the notion of: 'exclusive Government use' or 'general public use'. Moreover, the ability of courts to determine the adequacy of compensation is restricted in the legislation.[84] Article 47(2) of LUA provides that '[n]o court shall have jurisdiction to inquire into any question concerning or pertaining to the amount or adequacy of any compensation paid or to be paid under this Act'.[85] This appears to conflict with the provision of article 44(1)(b) of the Constitution.

But while being the primary legislation on land issues, relevant to situations of displacement due to development projects, for instance, the LUA does not essentially adopt a rights-based approach to expropriation by reinforcing the notion of rights or providing that compensation be adequate. While not also recognising compensation as a right, the constitutional right to property may not cover situations where those displaced are not property rights holder within the context of what is legally determinable.

3.4 Legal Stopgap: the Kampala Convention as supplementary law

Even while there is no specific legislation at the national level in the protection of IDPs, it is useful to emphasise that an immediate stopgap may be the application of the Kampala Convention in the furtherance of domestic response, and specifically in the furtherance of judicial protection of IDP rights. The argument here is that the Kampala Convention may still be applicable by virtue of its supplementary relationship with the African Charter on Human and Peoples' Rights (African Charter),[86] which has been domesticated in Nigeria. In the next sub-section, this chapter demonstrates this supplementary relationship as pre-existing and as such, the fundamental premise on which an application of the Kampala Convention within the Nigerian national framework is legitimate. But before this is done, it is useful to briefly reflect on the Kampala Convention.

3.4.1 The Kampala Convention as specific IDP law

With the realisation that Africa hosted some of the largest populations of persons displaced within state borders, the imperative for a regional solution to the issue of internal displacement emerged on the regional scene of priority action in 2004. Earlier, in 1998, the UN Guiding Principles on Internal Displacement (Guiding Principles) had been developed at the global level in response to the lacuna in protection and assistance of IDPs.[87]

Within the Great Lakes Region, a Protocol for the Protection and Assistance of IDPs was adopted to reinforce the applicability of the Guiding Principles within the region.[88] While this protocol, was indeed, a significant step towards creating a binding agreement on protection and assistance of IDPs, its focus on the Great Lakes Region made it inapplicable across the African region. In response to the legal gap on IDP issues, coupled with the understanding that the specific needs of these persons could not be addressed through the refugee regime, the African Union (AU) decided to develop a regional treaty on the issue and in 2009, the Kampala Convention was adopted in Uganda. The Kampala Convention are a set of 23 articles that aim to provide comprehensive protection for IDPs.[89] Its provisions notably reinforce prevention, protection, humanitarian assistance and durable solutions for IDPs.

The Kampala Convention commences with a preamble which underscores the pertinent motivation for the establishment of the treaty. Significantly, African states were motivated by the prevalence of internal displacement and the need to establish guidance on the protection and assistance of IDPs. Moreover, there were also human rights frameworks at the regional level that needed to be reinforced. Essentially, African states were mindful of the 'lack of a binding African and international legal and institutional framework specifically, for the prevention of internal displacement, and the protection and assistance to internally displaced persons'.[90]

Article 1 notably establishes key definitions in the Kampala Convention, significant among which is the definition of an IDP. While the definition adopts the language of the Guiding Principles on IDPs, it introduces non-state actors, harmful practices and armed groups. Moreover, it defines internal displacement as 'the involuntary or forced movement, evacuation or relocation of persons or groups of persons within internationally recognized state borders'.[91] The four strands of categorisation reinforce the nature of internal displacement as one that is perpetuated against the will of the displaced, but also that involves 'evacuation' or 'relocation', whether or not the will of those displaced are involved.

Article 2 sets out four primary objectives of the Kampala Convention. Notably, the Kampala Convention seeks to advance measures in addressing the root cause of internal displacement, establish a legal framework on IDP protection and assistance, provide a basis for solidarity, shared support and cooperation among states in addressing the issue of internal displacement, articulate the obligation of states in the context of internal displacement and also set out the responsibilities of various actors in the context of internal displacement, significantly also: non-state actors.[92]

Article 3 mandates the state to refrain from arbitrary displacement, marginalisation that may result in displacement and to ensure that the rights of IDPs are respected. There is also an emphasis on the accountability of non-state actors including multinationals. Moreover, states are to ensure that 'self-reliance and sustainable livelihoods' are promoted among IDPs.[93] Given that one of the pertinent aims of the Kampala Convention is to provide a legal text on which regional solutions can be sustained, including at the domestic level, states are required to incorporate their obligations in the treaty into national legislations through the enactment of laws and amendment of existing frameworks.[94] Moreover, institutional arrangements are to be made through the designation of national authorities for coordinating protection and assistance to IDPs.[95]

Article 4 emphasises the obligation to respect international legal provisions in preventing conditions that may result in arbitrary displacement. Moreover, there is an emphasis on cooperation with international organisations. Drawing on the importance of preventing arbitrary displacement, this provision further mandate states to 'declare as offences punishable by law acts of arbitrary displacement that amount to genocide, war crime sand crimes against humanity'.[96]

Article 5 reinforces the primary duty of states to protect and assist IDPs and the need for mutual cooperation. Moreover, it recognises displacement due to climate change and mandate states to take measures to 'protect and assist' displaced populations.[97] States are also to ensure unimpeded access for humanitarian actors in the protection of IDPs.[98] There is also an emphasis on the need for the state to ensure that 'armed groups act in conformity'.[99] However, the practical dimensions raise challenges.

Article 6 provides for the obligation of international organisations and humanitarian agencies. In this context, the Kampala Convention reinforces the need for these organisations and agencies to act in accordance with international standards and national laws within the states where they conduct activities. Notably, also, article 6 reinforces the need for these actors to respect the rights of IDPs in carrying out their activities. As with the Guiding Principles, the Kampala Convention emphasises the principles of humanity and impartiality[100] and further emphasises neutrality and independence.[101]

Article 7 articulates protection within the context of armed conflict. It begins with an emphasis that the provisions of article 7 'shall not, in any way whatsoever, be construed as affording legal status or legitimizing or recognizing armed groups'.[102] This provision is further accentuated in article 15(2) of the Kampala Convention, in relation to the provisions of the instrument.[103] Article 7(2) further reinforces the sovereignty of states and the prerogative of the state to 'maintain or re-establish law and order ... or to defend the national unity and territorial integrity of the State'.[104] The pertinence of international humanitarian law in the safeguard of IDPs is further accentuated in this provision.[105] Moreover, article 7(4) reinforces the criminal responsibility of members of armed groups 'for their acts which violate the rights of internally displaced persons under international law and national law'.[106] Specifically, article 7(5) prohibits armed groups from engaging in acts that affect protection and assistance of IDPs.[107]

Article 8 recognises the right of the AU to intervene in line with article 4(h) of the Constitutive Act in situations of 'war crimes', 'genocide' and 'crimes against humanity',[108] and further reinforces the right of states to request intervention as provided under article 4(j) of the Constitutive Act. Moreover, the AU is mandated to support state efforts towards protection and assistance of IDPs.[109]

Article 9 emphasises treatment standards during displacement.[110] It reinforces the protection of IDPs against discrimination, grave breaches, sexual and gender-based violence, extrajudicial killings and starvation.[111] Moreover, it outlines pertinent safeguards which states should be mindful of in fostering protection for IDPs including safety, family reunification and protection of property.[112]

Article 10 explicitly sets out obligations in the context of development projects requiring states to 'as much as possible' prevent this form of displacement and ensure stakeholders explore feasible alternatives 'with full information and consultation of persons likely to be displaced'.[113] Elsewhere it has been argued that this obligation requires states to ensure that feasible alternatives to development projects are considered with persons likely to be displaced in a bid to secure their free, prior and informed consent (FPIC) in order to avoid arbitrary displacement and that involuntary resettlement should be conceived as a last resort.[114] Also, states are to conduct prior impact assessments: socio-economic and environmental impacts.[115]

Article 11 emphasises durable solutions and require states to advance and create conditions 'for voluntary return, local integration or relocation on a sustainable basis and in circumstances of safety and dignity'.[116] Moreover, states must also ensure that IDPs are aided to make 'free and informed choice[s]' on these solutions.[117] Durable solutions are integral to the end of displacement. As such, it is imperative that states cooperate with various stakeholders 'in the course of finding and implementing solutions for sustainable return, local integration or relocation and long-term reconstruction'.[118] Developing mechanisms for dispute settlement, particularly with respect to the property of IDPs is integral to achieving these solutions.[119] This provision further places an emphasis on communities with specific attachment to land, requiring states to 'take all appropriate measures, whenever possible restore the lands' of these groups.[120] Indigenous peoples are particularly relevant in this context.

Article 12 reinforces the pertinence of compensation and require states to 'provide persons affected by displacement with effective remedies'.[121] This provision requires states to develop standards for compensation in line with relevant international frameworks.[122] It also reinforces the notion of reparations in situations where states 'refrain from protecting and assisting internally displaced persons in the event of natural disasters'.[123]

Article 13 mandates that states are to 'create and maintain an up-dated register' of IDPs. States are also to ensure that IDPs are issued relevant documentation in the 'enjoyment and exercise of their rights, such as passports, personal identification documents, civil certificates, birth certificates and marriage certificates'.[124] While the Guiding Principles provides that 'women and men' shall have equal rights to obtain the required documentation, the Kampala Convention further incorporates 'separated and unaccompanied children'.[125]

Article 14 incorporates monitoring mechanisms establishing a Conference of State Parties (COSP) and reinforcing the roles of the African Peer Review Mechanism and the African Commission on Human and Peoples' Rights (African Commission) in the context of state reporting.[126]

Articles 15 to 23 of the Kampala Convention incorporates final matters relating to application, signature, ratification and membership, entry into force, amendment and revisions, denunciation, saving clause, reservations, settlement of disputes and depository. Article 20 provides that the provision of the Kampala Convention should not be interpreted in a way that affects the right of IDPs to seek and be granted asylum and to provisions under human rights and humanitarian law instruments.[127] Moreover, article 21 of the Kampala Convention prohibits reservations 'that are incompatible with the object and purpose' of the treaty.[128]

In May 2012, Nigeria ratified the Kampala Convention.

3.4.2 The Kampala Convention as applicable supplementary law in Nigeria

A plethora of scholarly research has engaged the pertinence of the African Charter as the primary regional statement on human rights in Africa.[129] Extensively, also, there have been discussions on the domestic application of the African Charter in Nigeria through the domestication of the instrument by virtue of the African Charter on Human and Peoples' (Ratification and Enforcement) Act (ACHPR Act).[130] Indeed, in national jurisprudence, the applicability of the African Charter has been firmly established through decisions on human and peoples' rights at various court levels.

The Fundamental Rights Enforcement Procedure Rules (FREPR) further reinforces the applicability of the African Charter.[131] Through these rules (made pursuant to judicial powers under the Constitution), domestic courts are to apply the African Charter. But these rules are not just solely explicit on the applicability of the African Charter and this is emphatic in the objectives set out in the preamble which emphasises in paragraph 3 that[132]

The overriding objectives of these Rules are as follows:

(a) The Constitution, especially Chapter IV, as well as the African Charter, shall be expansively and purposely interpreted and applied, with a view to advancing and realising the rights and freedoms contained in them and affording the protections intended by them.

(b) For the purpose of advancing but never for the purpose of restricting the applicant's rights and freedoms, the Court shall respect municipal, regional and international bills of rights cited to it or brought to its attention or of which the Court is aware, whether these bills constitute instruments in themselves or form parts of larger documents like constitutions. Such bills include;

    (i) The African Charter on Human and Peoples' Rights and other instruments (including protocols) in the African regional human rights system,

(ii) The Universal Declaration of Human Rights and other instruments (including protocols) in the United Nations human rights system.

Consequently, by virtue of this provision, instruments under the regional and international human rights systems should guide the decisions of domestic courts. Notably, the emphasis of this provision is that fundamental rights are not solely those contained in the Constitution and the African Charter, but extensively relate to other instruments at various levels of governance. This makes sense. Not least, given the fact that Nigeria belongs to the international community and this reflects through its membership of the UN, the AU and the Economic Community of West African States (ECOWAS). Human rights norms within these strata are integral to the human rights corpus of the state. The innovation of the FREPR significantly demonstrates the position of the judiciary since the Supreme Court ruling in *Abacha v Fawehinmi*, where the Court emphasised (strictly with reference to section 12(1) of the Constitution), that international treaties that are not domesticated by the state are inapplicable.[133]

Indeed, this fundamental shift in legal thinking echoed in the FREPR rules and the progressions in the narrative of protection as reinforced by these rules demonstrate the fact that the human rights obligations of the state must be understood as a corpus that is complemented by other frameworks at levels beyond the domain of national normative regimes.

However, with respect to the Kampala Convention, there is a different stratum on which its applicability is reinforced and that is by virtue of article 66 of the African Charter. Article 66 of the African Charter provides that 'Special protocols or agreements may, if necessary, supplement the provisions of the present Charter'.[134] In explaining this provision, more concretely, it is pertinent to understand the notion of 'supplement'. In line with the ordinary meaning rule reinforced in the Vienna Convention on the Law of Treaties,[135] the notion of 'supplement' implies 'a thing that is added to something else to improve or complete it'[136] or a thing that 'gives extra information or deals with a special subject'.[137] In this context, a supplement provides further details or emphasis on a particular subject matter. Placed within the context of article 66 of the African Charter, what is reinforced is the fact that states may develop instruments to reinforce human and peoples' rights under the African Charter.[138] The yardstick for understanding if a protocol or agreement is contemplated within this text is to determine essentially if its focus is on the subject of the African Charter, i.e., human and peoples' rights. Since the formation of the African Charter, a plethora of normative frameworks have emerged as effective supplements to the regional human rights statement.[139] While the supplementary nature of these normative frameworks is often explicit in their titles as 'protocols' to the African Charter, there are others whose supplementary nature resonates from reference to the African Charter in their preambles and substantive provisions as the fundamental premise upon which their normative provisions find expression. Such is the case of the Kampala Convention, with its specific references to the African Charter. The African Commission has also accentuated this nexus in a General Comment on free movement of persons within the border of the state.[140] In an elaboration of the right to freedom of movement and residence within the borders of the state explicated provided under article 12(1) of the African Charter, the African Commission leveraged the Kampala Convention in defining protection and assistance in situations of internal displacement. This reinforces the fact that in understanding what the human rights corpus entails in the context of internal displacement, the Kampala Convention is instructive. As such, it is an effective supplement to the African Charter which sets out the regional human rights statement. Given the existence of this supplementary relationship, it is argued that the Kampala Convention may be applied in defining the parameters of protection and assistance to IDPs with reference to the African Charter.

While an application of this reasoning is yet to emerge in the jurisprudence, there is support for the Kampala Convention from a normative perspective at the domestic level. This is evident, for instance, in the extensive reflection of the Kampala Convention in the national IDP policy. As such, an application of the Kampala Convention as supplementary law in the context of the African Charter reinforces existing practice.

3.5 Conclusion

Evident from the general legal landscape is the fact that there are several norms relevant to IDP protection and assistance that cut across human rights, humanitarian law, migration, refugee law, environmental protection and land administration. As the apex law, the Constitution details a bill of rights that are applicable to IDPs. While these norms are relevant, on the whole, they appear fragmented. In providing specific IDP protection, this chapter identifies five options. However, as an immediate legal stopgap specifically in the judicial protection of IDP rights, this chapter argues that the Kampala Convention may be applied within the context of the African Charter which Nigeria has domesticated, as supplementary law.

Notes

1 See Chapter I of this Book (1.4.1 Primary Sources, Section A: Constitution).

2 The Constitution of the Federal Republic of Nigeria (1999), secs 33 (right to life) 41 (right to freedom of movement) & 42 (right to freedom from discrimination).
3 *Mustapha v Governor of Lagos State & Ors* (1987) LPELR-1931 (SC).
4 United Nations Guiding Principles on Internal Displacement (1998), principle 10.
5 As above, principle 10(2).
6 Constitution (n 2), sec 34.
7 *Rhodes & Anor v IGP & Ors* (2018) LPELR-44118 (CA), 10.
8 Guiding Principles (n 4), principle 8.
9 As above, principle 11.
10 *Aqua v Archibong & Ors* (2012) LPELR-9293(CA), 16.
11 Guiding Principles (n 4), principle 12(1).
12 As above.
13 As above.
14 As above, principle 12(3).
15 Constitution (n 2), sec 36.
16 *T.M. Orugbo & Anor v Bulara Una & Ors* (2002) LPELR-2778 (SC).
17 African Union Convention for the Protection and Assistance of Internally Displaced Persons in Africa (23 October 2009) (Kampala Convention), art 11(4).
18 UN Human Rights Council, *Report of the Special Rapporteur on the right to privacy – right to privacy*, UN Doc A/HRC/40/63 (16 October 2019), paras 8 & 10.
19 Constitution (n 2), sec 37.
20 *Nwali & Ebsiec & Ors* (2014) LPELR-23682 (CA), 35.
21 As above, 37.
22 Constitution (n 2), sec 38.
23 *Medical and Dental Practitioners Disciplinary tribunal v Okonkwo* (2001) LPELP-1856 (SC), 46; See also *Adamu & Ors v. Attorney General of Borno State* (1998) 8 NWLR 203.
24 Guiding Principles (n 4), principle 22(1).
25 Constitution (n 2), sec 39.
26 As above, sec 40.
27 *Okafor & Ors v Ntoka & Ors* (2017) LPELR-42794 (CA), 29.
28 Guiding Principles (n 4), principle 22(1)(c).
29 *Okafor v Lagos State Govt and Anor* (2016) LPELR-41066 (CA), 41.
30 Romola Adeola et al. 'A commentary on the African Commission's General Comment on the Right to Freedom of Movement and Residence under article 12(1) of the African Charter on Human and Peoples' Rights' (2021) *Journal of African Law* 1-21.
31 See General Comment No 5 on the African Charter on Human and Peoples' Rights: The Right to Freedom of Movement and Residence (article 12(1)) (2019).
32 *Lafia Local Govt v Executive Govt, Nasarawa State & Ors* (2012) LPELR-20602 (SC), 18–19.
33 *Kandix Ltd & Anor v AG & Commissioner for Justice, Cross River State & Anor* (2010) LPELR-4389 (CA), 8.
34 *Abacha v Fawehinmi* (2000) LPELR-14 (SC) 13.
35 See *Okogie v Attorney-General of Lagos State* (1981) 1 NCLR 218, 350.
36 *Centre for Oil Pollution Watch v Nigeria National Petroleum Corporation* (2019) 5 NWLR (Pt 1666) 518.

37 Constitution (n 2), sec 40.
38 *Centre for Oil Pollution Watch v Nigeria National Petroleum Corporation* (n 36).
39 As above.
40 See generally Eghosa O Ekhator 'The impact of the African Charter on Human and Peoples' Rights on domestic law: a case study of Nigeria' (2015) 41(2) *Commonwealth Law Bulletin* 253–270; Halima D Kutigi 'Towards justiciability of economic, social and cultural rights in Nigeria: a role for Canadian-Nigerian cooperation?' (2017) 4 *The Transnational Human Rights Review* 125–145.
41 *Mrs Georgina Ahamefule v Imperial Medical Centre & Dr Alex K Molokwu* Suit No. ID/1627/2000 (2012), 23,
42 *Odafe & Another v Attorney-General & Others* (2004) AHRLR 205 (NgHC 2004), para 38.
43 *Agemo & Others v Attorney General of Lagos State & Ors* Suit No. LD/4232MFHR/16 (2017), 4.
44 Child Rights Act (2003).
45 As above, sec 171(1) & (10).
46 As above.
47 See '11 states yet to domesticate Child Rights Act – Minister' *Premium Times (Nigeria)* 13 October 2020.
48 The recognition of internally displaced children is one of the areas in which the African Charter on the Rights and Welfare of the Child innovatively builds on the UN Convention on the Rights of the Child.
49 Discrimination against Persons with Disabilities (Prohibition) Act (2018).
50 Violence against Persons (Prohibition) Act (2015).
51 Cheluchi Onyemelukwe 'Legislating on violence against women: a critical analysis of Nigeria's recent Violence Against Persons (Prohibition) Act, 2015' (2016) 5(2) *DePaul Journal of Women, Gender and the Law* 1, 45.
52 Nigeria: Geneva Conventions Act (1960); See Geneva Convention for the Amelioration of the Condition of the Wounded and Sick in Armed Forces in the Field (12 August 1949) (First Geneva Convention); Geneva Convention for the Amelioration of the Condition of Wounded, Sick and Shipwrecked Members of Armed Forces at Sea (12 August 1949) (Second Geneva Convention); Geneva Convention Relative to the Treatment of Prisoners of War of 12 August 1949 (Third Geneva Convention); Geneva Convention Relative to the Protection of Civilian Persons in Time of War (12 August 1949) (Fourth Geneva Convention).
53 Protocol Additional to the Geneva Conventions of 12 August 1949 and Relating to the Protection of Victims of Non-international Armed Conflict (Additional Protocol II) (8 June 1977), art 17.
54 Jean-Marie Henckaerts 'Study on customary international humanitarian law: a contribution to the understanding and respect for the rule of law in armed conflict' (2005) 87(857) *International Review of the Red Cross* 175, 178
55 Common article 3 of the four Geneva Conventions of 1949.
56 Global Compact on Safe, Orderly and Regular Migration (2018).
57 National Migration Policy (2015).
58 See Romola Adeola 'Xenophobia and internal displacement in Africa: defining protection and assistance through the Kampala Convention' (2020) 27(4) *South African Journal of International Affairs* 493–510.
59 Land Use Act (1978); Petroleum Act (1969); Oil Pipelines Act (1956); Environmental Impact Assessment Act (1992); National Environmental Standards and Regulations Enforcement Act (2007).

60 National Environmental Standards and Regulations Enforcement Act (n 99), sec 27(1).
61 Environmental Impact Assessment Act (n 59), sec 2(1).
62 Oil Pipelines Act (n 59), sec 11(5).
63 National Emergency Management Agency (Establishment, Etc) Act (1999), art 6(2).
64 QueenEsther Iroanusi 'Senate laments lack of cooperation between NEMA, SEMA, others' *Premium Times* 10 November 2020.
65 Ibid.
66 Elizabeth Ferris 'Internal Displacement and the Right to Seek Asylum' (2008) 27(3) *Refugee Survey Quarterly* 76.
67 UN Convention Relating to the Status of Refugees (1951); OAU Convention Governing the Specific Aspects of Refugee Problems in Africa (1969) (OAU 1969 Refugee Convention).
68 OAU 1969 Refugee Convention (n 67), art 5.
69 See Jude O Ezeanokwasa et al 'A critique of the legal framework for arresting the threat of internal displacement of persons to Nigeria's national security' (2018) 9(2) *Nnamdi Azikiwe University Journal of International Law and Jurisprudence* 10, 16.
70 See Godwin O Nnadi et al 'The National Emergency Management Agency (NEMA) and the challenge of effective management of internally displaced persons in North Eastern Nigeria' (2020) 25(5) *IOSR Journal of Humanities and Social Science* 14–17.
71 See Jude O Ezeanokwasa et al 'A critique of the legal framework for arresting the threat of internal displacement of persons to Nigeria's national security' (2018) 9(2) *Nnamdi Azikiwe University Journal of International Law and Jurisprudence* 10, 16.
72 Constitution (n 2), sec 44(1)
73 Land Use Act (n 59), sec 1.
74 As above, sec 28(1).
75 As above, sec 29.
76 Nigerian Minerals and Mining Act (2007), sec 104.
77 *C.S.S Bookshop Ltd v Registered Trustees of Muslim Community in River States & Ors* (2006) LPELR-SC.307/2001.
78 Land Use Act (n 59), art 28(1)
79 Land Use Act (n 59), art 28(4)
80 *Aso Tim Doz Investment Company Limited v Abuja Markets Management Limited & Anor* (2016) LPELR-40367 (CA).
81 *Alhaji Wahabi Layiwola Olatunji v The Military Govenor of Oyo state & Ors* (1994) LPELR-14116 (CA).
82 *Ambo Wuyah v Jama'a Local Government, Kafanchan* (2011) LPELR-9078 (CA), 46.
83 *Goldmark Nigeria Limited & Ors v Ibafon Company Limited & Ors* (2012) LPELR-SC 421/2001, 71.
84 Land Use Act (n 59), art 51(1)(a).
85 Land Use Act (n 59), art 47(2).
86 African Charter on Human and Peoples' Rights (1981) (African Charter)
87 UN Commission on Human Rights, Addendum, 'Guiding Principles on Internal Displacement' *Report of the Representative of the Secretary-General, Mr. Francis M. Deng, submitted pursuant to Commission on Human Rights resolution 1997/39*, UN Doc. E/CN.4/1998/53/Add.2 (11 February 1998).

88 Protocol on the Protection and Assistance to Internally Displaced Persons, adopted by International Conference on the Great Lakes (30 November 2006).
89 See Kampala Convention (n 17); Mehari T Maru *The Kampala Convention and its contribution to international law: legal analyses and interpretations of the African Union Convention for the Protection and Assistance of Internally Displaced Persons* (Eleven Publishing, 2014); Cristiano D'Orsi 'Strengths and weaknesses in the protection of the internally displaced persons in Sub-Saharan Africa' (2012) 28(1) *Connecticut Journal of International Law* 73; Allehone M Abebe *The Emerging Law on Forced Migration in Africa: Development and Implementation of the Kampala Convention on Internal Displacement* (Routledge, 2016).
90 Kampala Convention (n 17), para 14 of the Preamble.
91 As above, art 1(l).
92 As above, art 2.
93 As above, art 3(1)(k).
94 As above, art 3(2).
95 As above, art 3(2).
96 As above, art 4(6).
97 As above, art 5(4).
98 Article 5(7) of the Kampala Convention provides that: 'States Parties shall take necessary steps to effectively organize, relief action that is humanitarian, and impartial in character, and guarantee security. States Parties shall allow rapid and unimpeded passage of all relief consignments, equipment and personnel to internally displaced persons. States Parties shall also enable and facilitate the role of local and international organizations and humanitarian agencies, civil society organizations and other relevant actors, to provide protection and assistance to internally displaced persons. States Parties shall have the right to prescribe the technical arrangements under which such passage is permitted'. See Kampala Convention (n 17), art 5(7).
99 Kampala Convention (n 17), art 5(11).
100 Guiding Principles (n 4), art 24.
101 Kampala Convention (n 17), art 6(3).
102 As above, art 7.
103 Article 15(2) of the Kampala Convention provides that 'States Parties agree that nothing in this Convention shall be construed as affording legal status or legitimizing or recognizing armed groups and that its provisions are without prejudice to the individual criminal responsibility of their members under domestic or international criminal law'. Kampala Convention (n 17), art 15(2).
104 Kampala Convention (n 17), art 7(2).
105 As above, art 7(3).
106 As above, art 7(4).
107 Particularly, article 7(5) of the Kampala Convention provides that: 'Members of armed groups shall be prohibited from: (a) Carrying out arbitrary displacement; (b) Hampering the provision of protection and assistance to internally displaced persons under any circumstances; (c) Denying internally displaced persons the right to live in satisfactory conditions of dignity, security, sanitation, food, water, health and shelter; and separating members of the same family; (d) Restricting the freedom of movement of internally displaced persons within and outside their areas of residence; (e) Recruiting children or requiring or permitting them to take part in hostilities under any circumstances; (f)

Forcibly recruiting persons, kidnapping, abduction or hostage taking, engaging in sexual slavery and trafficking in persons especially women and children; (g) Impeding humanitarian assistance and passage of all relief consignments, equipment and personnel to internally displaced persons; (h) Attacking or otherwise harming humanitarian personnel and resources or other materials deployed for the assistance or benefit of internally displaced persons and shall not destroy, confiscate or divert such materials; and (i)Violating the civilian and humanitarian character of the places where internally displaced persons are sheltered and shall not infiltrate such places'. See Kampala Convention (n 17), art 5(7).

108 Kampala Convention (n 17), art 8(1); for discussion on article 4(h) of the AU Constitutive Act and on the principle of responsibility to protect, see Dan Kuwali *The responsibility to protect: implementation of article 4(h) intervention* (Martinus Nijhoff, 2011); Dan Kuwali and Frans Viljoen (eds) *Africa and the responsibility to protect: article 4(h) of the African Union Constitutive Act* (Routledge, 2014); Alex J Bellamy *The responsibility to protect: a defense* (Oxford University Press, 2015).

109 Specifically article, article 8(3) mandate states to support state efforts towards IDP protection and assistance and in this regard, '(a) Strengthen the institutional framework and capacity of the African Union with respect to protection and assistance to internally displaced persons; (b) Coordinate the mobilisation of resources for protection and assistance to internally displaced persons; (c) Collaborate with international organizations and humanitarian agencies, civil society organizations and other relevant actors in accordance with their mandates, to support measures taken by States Parties to protect and assist internally displaced persons. (d) Cooperate directly with African States and international organizations and humanitarian agencies, civil society organizations and other relevant actors, with respect to appropriate measures to be taken in relation to the protection of and assistance to internally displaced persons; (e) Share information with the African Commission on Human and Peoples' Rights on the situation of displacement, and the protection and assistance accorded to internally displaced persons in Africa; and (f) Cooperate with the Special Rapporteur of the African Commission on Human and Peoples' Rights for Refugees, Returnees, IDPs and Asylum Seekers in addressing issues of internally displaced persons.

110 Kampala Convention (n 17), art 9.

111 As above, art 9(1).

112 As above, art 9(2).

113 As above, art 10(2).

114 Romola Adeola *Development-induced displacement and human tights: the Kampala Convention* (Routledge, 2021).

115 Kampala Convention (n 17), art 10(3).

116 As above, art 11(1).

117 As above, art 11(2).

118 As above, art 11(3).

119 As above, art 11(4).

120 As above, art 11(5).

121 As above, art 12(1).

122 As above, art 12(2).

123 As above, art 12(3).

124 As above, art 13(2).
125 As above, art 13(4).
126 As above, art 14.
127 As above, art 20.
128 As above, art 21.
129 Oji U Umozurike *The African Charter on Human and Peoples' Rights* (Martinus Nijhoff, 1997); Fatsah Ouguergouz *African Charter on Human and Peoples' Rights: a comprehensive agenda for human dignity and sustainable democracy in Africa* (Martinus Nijhoff Publishers, 2003); Kofi O Kufuor *The African human rights system: origin and evolution* (Palgrave Macmillan, 2010); Frans Viljoen *International human rights law in Africa* (Oxford University Press, 2012); Bonny Ibhawoh *Human rights in Africa* (Cambridge University Press, 2018); Frans Viljoen 'Africa's contribution to the development of international human rights and humanitarian law' in Eunice N Sahle (ed) *Human rights in Africa: contemporary debates and struggles* (Palgrave Macmillan, 2019) 203; Rachel Murray *The African Charter on Human and Peoples' Rights: a commentary* (Oxford University Press, 2019).
130 African Charter on Human and Peoples' (Ratification and Enforcement) Act (1983); Chudi N Ojukwu 'Enforcement of the African Charter on Human and Peoples' Rights as a domestic law in Nigeria' (2000) 25(4) *International Legal Practitioner* 140; Frans Viljoen 'Application of the African Charter on Human and Peoples' Rights by domestic courts in Africa' (1999) 43(1) *Journal of African Law* 1; Muyiwa Adigun 'The implementation of the African Charter on Human and Peoples' Rights and the Convention on the Rights of the Child in Nigeria: the creation of irresponsible parents and dutiful children?' (2019) 51 *The Journal of Legal Pluralism and Unofficial Law* 320.
131 Fundamental Rights Enforcement Procedure Rules (2009); Anthony O Nwafor 'Enforcing fundamental rights in Nigerian courts – processes and challenges' (2009) 4 *African Journal of Legal Studies* 1; Abiola Sanni 'Fundamental Rights Enforcement Procedure Rules, 2009 as a tool for the enforcement of the African Charter on Human and Peoples' Rights in Nigeria: the need for far-reaching reform' (2011) 11 *African Human Rights Law Journal* 511.
132 Fundamental Rights Enforcement Procedure Rules (n 131).
133 Constitution (n 2), sec 12(1).
134 African Charter on Human and Peoples' Rights (n 86), art 66.
135 Vienna Convention on the Law of Treaties 1969 1155 UNTS 331 (VCLT), art 31(1).
136 'Supplement' *Oxford Learner's Dictionaries* https://www.oxfordlearnersdict ionaries.com/definition/english/supplement_1?q=supplement (accessed 6 May 2020).
137 Ibid.
138 Ibid.
139 African Charter on the Rights and Welfare of the Child (1990); Protocol to the African Charter on Human and Peoples' Rights on the Rights of Women in Africa (2003); Protocol to the African Charter on Human and Peoples' Rights on the Rights of Older Persons (2016); Protocol to the African Charter on Human and Peoples' Rights on the Rights of Persons with Disabilities in Africa (2018).
140 See General Comment No 5 (n 31).

4 Reflection on the National Policy on internally displaced persons, 2021

4.1 Introduction

While there is no specific legislation on internally displaced persons (IDPs) in Nigeria, a National Policy on IDPs (the Policy) was adopted in 2021.[1] Notably, the Policy reinforces normative frameworks at the global and regional levels. Second, it is emphatic on rights and as such adopts a rights-based approach. Third, it reinforces the responsibilities of armed groups, which is significant given the humanitarian context in Nigeria. Fourth, it addresses the challenge of coordination which has been a bane in humanitarian interventions. This chapter examines the content of the Policy, reflecting on its provisions.

4.2 Brief background

Specifically on internal displacement, there have been attempts towards the development of normative frameworks for nearly two decades. One of the earliest moves towards this process followed the establishment of a Presidential Committee on Internally Displaced Persons (the Presidential Committee).[2] The Presidential Committee was established in 2004 and was mandated with the development of a policy framework on internal displacement.[3] A draft policy was developed in 2006 and tabled before the Federal Executive Council in 2007;[4] however, it was not adopted at the time. While the policy was initiated by the Presidential Committee, the policy development process was subsequently taken on by the National Commission for Refugees, Migrants and IDPs (NCFRMI) and the policy was subsequently revised between 2009 and 2012 to reflect the African Union Convention on the Protection and Assistance of Internally Displaced Persons in Africa (Kampala Convention).[5] However, the Policy remained a draft, although several commitments towards the development of a normative framework continued. With the establishment of a specific Ministry of Humanitarian Affairs, Disaster Management and Social Development (FMHADMSD) in

DOI: 10.4324/9781003146025-4

2019,[6] the policy development process was significantly revived and eventually tabled before the Federal Executive Council in 2021.[7] The Policy was adopted subject to the finalisation of comments which was eventually concluded.

4.3 The Policy framework

The Policy is divided into six chapters. The first part gives an introduction, reflecting on the contextual background and providing a definition of key terms utilised in the framework. The second part reflects the thrust of the policy specifically providing for the policy framework and scope, policy vision and mission, policy goal and objectives and policy guiding principles. The third part examines the rights and obligations of IDPs while the fourth part considers the responsibilities of government, humanitarian agencies, host communities and armed groups to IDPs. The fifth part explores the policy implementation framework and strategies. The sixth part considers funding, monitoring, evaluation, and policy review. This section examines the various provisions.

4.3.1 Chapter One: introduction

The first chapter of the Policy provides an introduction reflecting on the contextual background and situation analysis and further providing a definition of key terms used in the policy.

4.3.1.1 Contextual background and situation analysis

In this section, the Policy identifies specific challenges in the context of protection and assistance to IDPs. It is observed that 'there is no reliable database for the comprehensive profile of IDPs in Nigeria'.[8] Moreover, it further identifies that '[m]ost of the IDPs were displaced between 2014 and 2015 (68.7%) with 21.5% displaced between 2016 and 2021'.[9] While Nigeria has ratified the Kampala Convention, the fact that a normative lacuna existed was observed. The Policy observes that

> [i]n the absence of a policy framework on internal displacement in Nigeria, the response to the plight of IDPs has remained largely fragmented and uncoordinated; and the response to the root causes of internal displacement, has been very poor and ineffective.[10]

The essence of the Policy against a broader regional context within the Economic Community of West African States (ECOWAS) region also resonates.[11] In 2011, for instance, the First Ministerial Conference on Humanitarian Assistance and Internal Displacement in West Africa organized by the ECOWAS was held under the leadership of the Nigerian government.[12]

The Policy further identifies causes of internal displacement in Nigeria emphasising that 'most of the incidences of internal displacement occur because of violent conflicts with ethnic, religious and/or political undertones'.[13] Displacement due to natural disasters and development projects are observed. The Policy further emphasises displacement due to election violence emphasising that[14]

[a]nalysts have always expressed fears that the level of conflict and the attendant level of internal displacement, may increase each time general elections draw nearer. These fears were confirmed when the National Emergency Management Agency (NEMA) reported that about 65,000 persons were displaced internally due to 2011 post-election violence spread across six Northern states including Bauchi, Kaduna, Kano, Niger, Katsina and Sokoto.

Moreover, the Policy observes the evident link between good governance/ democratic deficits and displacement episodes, noting that 'people's vulnerability to internal displacement in Nigeria is not only due to natural and man-made disasters, armed conflict, and ethno-religious-political conflicts but is also worsened by extreme poverty, lack of equal access to socioeconomic resources and balanced development, high unemployment rate among able-bodied and frustrated youths.'[15] It further recognises that one of the factors that worsen the plight of IDPs is the inadequacy of processes for fostering informed decision-making for IDPs towards securing durable solutions to the displacement situation.[16]

The fact that the Policy has emerged as a response to internal displacement is reinforced as a

demonstration of political will to providing durable solutions to the plight of IDPs and a practical admission of the fact that ensuring IDP protection and assistance primarily lies with national authorities whose mandate and obligation it is to protect and care for them.[17]

The normative grounding of the IDP policy is also reinforced, significant among which are: section 14(2)(b) of the 1999 Nigerian Constitution which emphasises that the primary purpose of the state shall be 'security and welfare of the people';[18] articles 3(2) (development of a normative framework),

4 (protection from arbitrary displacement) and 7 (armed conflict) of the Kampala Convention.[19]

The Policy further underscores the impact of internal displacement on IDPs and host communities. For IDPs, displacement has the effect of disruption, given that these persons are uprooted from their homes or places of habitual residences. Moreover, displacement may result in a lack of access to basic services and exposes IDPs to increased vulnerability and risks. In displacement, families may be separated and access to justice may be daunting. The Policy further observes that[20]

> Even when the situation of most IDPs improves, potentially durable solutions have remained out of the reach of specific groups with particular needs or vulnerabilities. These include the elderly or sick people, widows barred from recovering the property they had lived on, or members of minorities facing discrimination, marginalization and exclusion or whose livelihoods depend on attachment to their areas of origin or settlement. For such groups, strategies or incentives that had encouraged others to move towards a durable solution may not have been effective or accessible, and the tailored support they needed to rebuild their lives may not be available.

The Policy observes that in host communities, existing services may be overstretched. And local integration for IDPs in such situations may be daunting.[21] However, it is significant that the Policy recognises that the presence of IDPs in host communities can also result in improved care for host communities. The Policy observes that[22]

> experience from the North-East of Nigeria has shown that host communities have also benefitted from the presence of IDPs in their communities in the areas of improved healthcare; for instance, the expansion of hospital facilities and personnel through the intervention of the Government and Non-Government Agencies.

4.3.1.2 Definition of key terms

The Policy defines 38 terms integral to an understanding of the Policy provisions.[23] Significantly, it draws on the Guiding Principles and the Kampala Convention in its explication of terms – for instance, in the definition of arbitrary displacement, internal displacement and IDPs. Other terms are also drawn from global and regional frameworks such as armed conflict and armed groups. In its definition of armed conflict, the Policy delineates between international and non-international armed conflicts providing that[24]

armed conflict means *international armed conflict*, which is the resort to armed force on the territory of another State without its consent; as well as *non-international armed conflict*, which is protracted armed confrontations of a minimum level of intensity occurring between governmental armed forces and the forces of one or more organized armed groups, or between such groups arising on the territory of a State.

While it defines protection reflecting on the guidance of the Inter-Agency Standing Committee on Internally Displaced Persons Protection Policy (1999),[25] it omits an insight on humanitarian assistance which could be useful in interventions by stakeholders. It is interesting that it advances a definition of vulnerability emphasising that it

involves a combination of factors that determine the degree to which someone's life, livelihood, property and other assets are susceptible to risk caused by a discrete and identifiable event (or series or cascade of such events) in nature and society.[26]

However, the Policy does not seem to define the notion of deprivation. Notably, however, it provides an insight into the notion of livelihood as[27]

the combination of the resources used and the activities undertaken in order to live. The resources might consist of individual skills and abilities (human capital), land, savings and equipment (natural, financial and physical capital, respectively), and formal support groups or informal networks that assist in the activities being undertaken (social capital).

It is crucial to mention that there are specific innovations of this Policy section such as the definition of specific root causes of internal displacement including development-induced displacement (DID), conflict-induced displacement and disaster-induced displacement.

The Policy defines DID as a 'situation where people are compelled to move as a result of policies and projects implemented to supposedly enhance "development"'.[28] The provision further goes on to give examples of these as: 'large-scale infrastructure projects such as dams, roads, ports, airports, refineries and oil and gas installations'.[29] The clarity afforded by this definition is pertinent in delineating DID from other root causes and specifically identifying situations that may come within the context of this root cause of internal displacement. With respect to conflict-induced displacement, the national policy provides a broad description in providing that this is[30]

> displacement resulting from people being forced to flee their homes for one or more reasons including armed conflict, communal conflicts, generalized violence, etc. and where the state authorities are unable or unwilling to protect them.

The Policy further defines 'disaster' and specifically also 'disaster-induced displacement'. Disaster-induced displacement is defined as 'displacement of people caused by natural hazards, disasters (floods, volcanoes, landslides, earthquakes), environmental change (deforestation, desertification, land degradation, global warming) and human-made induced disasters (industrial accidents, radioactivity)'.[31] However, the Policy does not provide an insight into climate change and harmful practices which are also evident root causes of internal displacement.

4.3.2 Chapter Two: Policy thrust

The second chapter of the Policy reflects on the framework and scope, vision and mission, goals and objectives and guiding principles of the Policy.

From the onset, the Policy emphasises the fact that it sets out a framework for 'national responsibility towards prevention and protection of citizens and, in some cases, non-citizens, from incidences of arbitrary and other forms of internal displacement',[32] while also meeting 'assistance and protection needs during displacement'[33] and to ensure 'rehabilitation, reintegration and relocation after displacement'.[34] The ambition of the Policy in significantly addressing situations of internal displacement is evidently spelt out in this section. As a rights-based framework,[35] the Policy seeks to address all causes of internal displacement, groups in internal displacement, needs of IDPs, phases of displacement, levels of displacement, affected areas, rights of IDPs, obligations of state and non-state actors.

The Policy envisions proactivity in addressing situations of internal displacement and iterates the fact that it seeks to set out 'a framework for national accountability and responsibility to protect, promote and fulfil the rights of internally displaced persons, families and host communities'.[36] While seeking to strengthen institutional capacities towards protecting IDPs and achieving durable solutions, the Policy is guided by some cardinal principles which are split into two groups: general and humanitarian principles. With respect to general principles, the Policy emphasises respect for sovereignty, gender equality, empowerment, participation and accountability.[37]

Within the sub-set of humanitarian principles are principles of humanity, neutrality, impartiality and non-discrimination, independence and protection from harm and abuse.[38]

4.3.3 Rights and obligations of IDPs

This section of the Policy sets out the rights and obligations of IDPs. The Policy iterates that '[a]ll rights contained in the Constitution of Nigeria, statutes and domesticated sub-regional, regional and international human rights and humanitarian treaties, which all citizens of Nigeria are entitled to, shall be applicable to all internally displaced persons in Nigeria'.[39] It further emphasises the right of IDPs to leave their country of origin and seek asylum in another country, as well as the right to 'request and receive protection and assistance from the state and local authorities'.[40] It emphasises that IDPs 'shall not be punished or persecuted for making such a request',[41] and iterates the right of IDPs who are vulnerable to 'receive protection and assistance required by their condition or special needs'.[42] The Policy emphasises the right to protection from displacement, protection during and after displacement and rights in the context of durable solutions. Notably, it is detailed on the rights of various categories of IDPs including children, women, persons with disabilities, IDPs living with HIV and the elderly.

With respect to children, the Policy provides detailed guidance emphasising the right of the child to name and nationality, family reunification, resettlement in a safe space, education and protection from child labour. While it emphasises the best interests of the child, specifically for orphaned children, the Policy does not significantly spotlight this principle as an overarching norm in the furtherance of the rights of children. However, it is significant that the Policy emphasises that internally displaced children 'shall, in particular, enjoy their rights under the Child Rights Act and similar laws enacted at the State and local government levels'.[43] The Policy further recognises intersectionality, seeking to protect 'children in exceptionally difficult circumstances' and in this regard emphasises that 'a special regime shall be established for the protection of children in such difficult circumstances which shall include but not be limited to orphans, children with health challenges and children with disabilities'.[44]

With respect to women, the Policy emphasises the protection of women against 'indignity' and iterates that internally displaced women 'shall not be subjected to any form of indignity; including beating, forced labour, sexual abuse or exploitation, or forceful stripping either for medical examination or other reasons whatsoever without her consent.'[45] The Policy further reinforces the protection of women from situations of forced marriage and seeks to reiterate the freedom of women to engage in financial and economic livelihood opportunities. Significantly, the Policy further emphasises that '[i]nternally displaced women shall be encouraged and entitled to hold any position of authority in IDPs leadership committees without any form of discrimination, ensuring at least 50% representative roles or other leadership positions'.[46] However, the Policy does not significantly stress intersectionality such as specific protection for pregnant or elderly women. In detailing protection for persons with disabilities, the Policy emphasises the need to remove barriers that may impede on the enjoyment of rights for persons with disabilities. It further emphasises protection for children with disabilities and institutionally reinforces the fact that the

> National Commission for Persons with Disabilities together with the protection sector lead agencies established by this policy through the sectoral approach should be empowered to carry out activities aimed at restoring the dignity and protection of persons living with disabilities.[47]

For IDPs living with HIV, the Policy emphasises non-discrimination and emphasises the need for various sectors in the Policy to 'mainstream HIV and AIDs into their protection and assistance interventions'. Moreover, the Policy emphasises the need for IDPs living with HIV to have access to water, sanitation and hygiene, adequate care and psychosocial support and anti-retroviral drugs. The Policy also iterates that women living with HIV should have 'access to prevention-of-mother-to-child services and information, including family planning, treatment and infant feeding options'. Significantly, the Policy further emphasises the need for confidentiality of data for IDPs living with HIV.

For the elderly, the Policy observes that during displacement older persons are often left behind. It observes that 'families have to make the painful choice of leaving them behind as opportunity cost for saving children and younger people'.[48] The Policy further observes the gap in humanitarian intervention for elderly persons and the fact that 'their needs are largely unmet in collective shelters and resettlement camps'.[49] The Policy reinforces the need to take into account the vulnerability of the elderly and specifically requires that those left behind are reunited with their families 'as soon as possible', provided with adequate social support, relevant psychosocial support, post-traumatic counselling and palliative care.[50] Moreover, the Policy emphasises the need to ensure that the basic needs of the elderly during displacement are provided, special queues are made at points of food distribution and in health centres. The Policy further iterates that there should be 'social spaces' within camps, shelters and in host communities where the elderly can socialise, gain skills and obtain livelihood support. Significantly, the Policy further emphasises intersectionality, reinforcing the need to ensure that elderly women are 'protected from physical and sexual abuse, including all forms of gender-based violence and discrimination'.[51]

While the specific mention of these groups is significant, the Policy, however, omits specific mention of groups such as persons living with albinism and young persons. With respect to obligations, the Policy reinforces individual criminal responsibility and emphasises that IDPs should '[r]espect the culture and norms of host communities'[52] and 'abide by rules and regulations in collective settlements'.[53]

4.3.4 Responsibilities of government, humanitarian agencies, host communities and armed groups to IDPs

Significantly, the Policy emphasises the responsibility of the state and various groups relevant to situations of internal displacement. In the context of state obligation, the Policy emphasises the obligations to respect, protect and fulfil rights and draws from the Kampala Convention significantly with respect to the obligation of states to '[r]espect and ensure respect for their obligations under international human rights and humanitarian law, so as to prevent and avoid conditions that might lead to the arbitrary displacement of persons'.[54] While these are imperative, an evident gap relates to the obligation to promote the rights of IDPs. This is crucial in order to foster awareness among various stakeholders that may be involved in the protection and assistance of IDPs, among host communities and the general public, and among IDPs themselves, who may not significantly be aware of their rights in the context of displacement. Notably, the Policy further emphasises the need for the state to create 'a legal framework for upholding the rights of internally displaced persons including domestication and implementation of the Kampala Convention'.[55]

With respect to humanitarian agencies, the Policy generally emphasises the need for compliance with law and policy guidelines, the code of conduct and standard operating procedures and adherence to minimum standards, specifically the Core Sphere 'process and people Minimum Standards'.[56] The obligation in article 6 of the Kampala Convention relating to humanitarian actors is significantly echoed.

The Policy further sets out the rights and obligations of host communities, recognising the need to ensure the adoption of 'community-based approaches to internal displacement response that take into consideration the responsibilities of government and humanitarian agencies towards protection and assistance of IDP host communities and the full realisation of their human rights based on adequate needs assessment'.[57]

The Policy further recognises the need to ensure that armed groups do not carry out arbitrary displacement and emphasises the provision of article 7 of the Kampala Convention that reinforces the provision of international humanitarian law.

4.3.5 Policy implementation framework and strategies

In the furtherance of implementation, the Policy provides for a framework in the realisation of coordination and collaboration for the realisation of its provisions.

4.3.5.1 Broad strategies

In the realisation of its provisions, the Policy emphasises the development of a Comprehensive Displacement Management and Implementation Framework (CDMIF) and a 'comprehensive monitoring and evaluation framework with clear indicators to assess the progress in the implementation of the CDMIF'.[58] As part of the broad strategies, the Policy further emphasises strategies for prevention of internal displacement, protection and assistance of IDPs during displacement, rehabilitation of IDPs, durable solutions and sensitisation of communities in areas of return, relocation or local integration.

4.3.5.2 Achieving durable solutions to internal displacement

Given the importance of durable solutions to the realisation of IDP protection, the Policy further emphasises strategies for achieving durable solutions drawing on the Inter-Agency Standing Committee's Framework on Durable Solutions for IDPs.[59] Notably, the Policy emphasises that 'a durable solution is achieved when internally displaced persons no longer have any specific assistance and protection needs that are linked to their displacement and can enjoy their human rights without discrimination on account of their displacement'.[60] In this section, the Policy further reflects on the 'rehabilitation of the environment of host communities'.[61] However, the provisions in this section do not appear to cohere with the heading. Nevertheless, it is significant that the Policy provides in this section that[62]

The search for any of these durable solutions for internally displaced persons should be understood as a gradual, often long-term process of reducing displacement-specific needs and ensuring the enjoyment of human rights without discrimination.

Achieving durable solutions is, therefore, a complex process that addresses human rights, humanitarian, development, reconstruction and peace-building challenges, requiring the coordinated and timely engagement of different actors.

In seeking durable solutions, intervening agencies must avoid creating dependence and facilitate return as soon as conditions permit, by providing aid that is adequate but not creating living conditions of a higher standard than those in the IDPs' areas of origin which could become an incentive for not seeking voluntary return or relocation.

4.3.5.3 Institutional mechanism for coordination and collaboration

This section of the Policy emphasises the institutional mechanism for the furtherance of coordination and collaboration. Notably, it recognises the fact that before the formation of the FMHADMSD,

> an assessment of internal displacement response coordination mechanism in Nigeria showed that there were systematic gaps in assistance, protection and some other sectors for intervention at the various phases of displacement, and most agencies take unilateral and mandate-based decisions on their involvement which usually lack accountability.[63]

Notably, the role of the FMHADMSD as the institution to 'provide overall leadership for the coordinating of all humanitarian issues, formulation of policy frameworks and its implementations'[64] is clearly emphasised.

4.3.5.4 Broad institutional framework and implementing agencies

The Policy specifically sets out pertinent institutions that should integrate IDP protection and assistance in their 'core mandates', and these include[65]

1. The Federal Ministry of Humanitarian Affairs, Disaster Management and Social Development;
2. The Federal Ministry of Women Affairs;
3. The Federal Ministry of Information and Culture;
4. The Federal Ministry of Water Resources;
5. The Federal Ministry of Health;
6. The Ministry of Communication and Digital Economy;
7. The National Commission for Refugees, Migrants and Internally Displaced Persons;

8. The National Emergency Management Agency;
9. The State Emergency Management Agencies;
10. The National Human Rights Commission;
11. The Office of the National Security Adviser;
12. The Nigeria Security and Civil Defence Corps;
13. The National Agency for the Prohibition of Trafficking in Persons;
14. The Institute for Peace and Conflict Resolution;
15. The International Institute for Tropical Agriculture;
16. The Ministry of Environment;
17. The Ministry of Youth and Sports Development;
18. UN agencies;
19. The Nigerian Red Cross Society;
20. The National Population Commission;
21. The Ministry of Budget and National Planning;
22. The Small and Medium Enterprises Development Agency;
23. Civil society organisations;
24. Private sector institutions/organisations;
25. International humanitarian organisations;
26. The mass media;
27. The Ministry of Interior;
28. The Ministry of Justice;
29. The Industrial Training Fund;
30. The National Directorate of Employment;
31. The Special Duties Office (OSGF);
32. The National Drug Law Enforcement Agency;
33. The Bank of Agriculture;
34. The Bank of Industry;
35. Relevant sectors, ministries, departments and agencies; and
36. The Nigeria Police Force.

While the specific listing of these institutions is useful, it would have been better for the Policy to spotlight specific roles that these institutions should play in the realisation of IDP protection and assistance as a key pointer in the formulation of policies and normative strategies for IDPs. Moreover, the Policy does not mention other crucial actors such as the Nigerian Immigration Services, the military and other crucial ministries such as Finance, and Works and Housing.

4.3.5.5 Framework for international cooperation

The Policy provides for a cooperation strategy between the Nigerian government, with primary responsibility to protect IDPs, and 'international humanitarian agencies, donor partners, international non-governmental organisations and human rights institutions'.[66] It reinforces the role of the state through the FMHADMSD and emphasises the need for the state to[67]

1. Liaise directly with the Humanitarian Country Team (HCT) established by the United Nations System in Nigeria through the office of the Resident/Humanitarian Coordinator to develop integrated plans of action in the event of displacement;
2. Seek for technical assistance and support from the international humanitarian community including humanitarian agencies; development partners, international non-governmental organisations and human rights agencies, especially where national capacity for providing adequate protection and assistance to affected persons and communities in any of the phases of internal displacement is insufficient;
3. Cooperate, where appropriate, with IDP focal points of ECOWAS, the African Union and international organizations or humanitarian agencies and civil society organizations, in providing protection and assistance as well as finding and implementing durable solutions for sustainable return, local integration, relocation and long-term reconstruction;
4. Request for activation of global humanitarian clusters of the international humanitarian community when the situation exceeds local capacity to respond;
5. Designate sectoral focal persons who shall liaise directly with corresponding national sector leads and global cluster leads of the international humanitarian agencies and donors to ensure coordinated response to all phases of internal displacement from pre-emergency to durable solutions;
6. Cooperate with humanitarian agencies, civil society organizations and other relevant actors to devise early warning systems, in areas of potential displacement, establish and implement disaster risk reduction strategies, emergency and disaster preparedness and management measures and, where necessary, provide immediate protection and assistance to internally displaced persons;
7. Recognise the right of international humanitarian organizations and other appropriate actors to offer their services in support of the internally displaced. To this regard, the government shall not regard such offers of assistance as unfriendly acts or interference in internal affairs and shall consider them in good faith to the extent to which they do not undermine the country's sovereignty;
8. Provide unrestricted access and not withhold consent thereto without serious and objective reasons, and accept external assistance, particularly when local agencies and relevant authorities concerned are

unable or unwilling to provide the required humanitarian assistance or protection;

9. Liaise with all national authorities concerned to grant and facilitate for international humanitarian organizations and other appropriate actors, in the exercise of their respective mandates, rapid and unimpeded access to internally displaced persons to assist in their rehabilitation, return, relocation and local integration;

10. Respect the independence and operational autonomy of international humanitarian actors, and shall not unduly interfere with their internal affairs and modus operandi, as long as they operate within the ambits of local and international laws.

It further emphasises the role of regional, international humanitarian and development actors providing that[68]

Where international humanitarian agencies, development partners and International Non-governmental Organisations (INGOs) are involved in providing assistance and protection in the event of internal displacement, they shall:

1. Collaborate directly with the corresponding national sectoral leads established under the sectoral approach in this policy to execute actions in a way that strengthens local capacity and maximises use of available human, financial and material resources;

2. Give due regard to the protection needs and human rights of IDPs and commit to the principles underlying this policy including the principles of humanity and humanitarian imperative, neutrality, impartiality and non-discrimination, independence and respect for national sovereignty; and

3. Commit to the obligations of humanitarian actors prescribed by the Kampala Convention (Article 6) and responsibilities defined in this policy (Section 4.2). Fundamental to this is compliance with the national and international laws and guidelines for protection and assistance of IDPs, adoption of international best practices, adherence to internationally acceptable codes of conduct and standard operating procedures for protection and delivery of humanitarian assistance services, and compliance with the Sphere Core Minimum Standards for humanitarian assistance across all sectors.

However, this section of the Policy seems to omit to mention other actors including the private sector, international service providers and faith-based organisations who are also key partners in the protection and assistance of IDPs.

4.3.5.6 *Legal framework*

The Policy emphasises the fact that it draws on human rights and the humanitarian obligations of Nigeria as given in the Constitution, relevant legislation and treaties that have been ratified and domesticated. The Policy further emphasises the need for the state to take specific actions geared towards strengthening the legal framework, including:[69]

1. Domesticate the Kampala Convention on the Protection and Assistance of IDPs;
2. Comply with its international obligations under the Kampala Convention and other relevant human rights and humanitarian law instruments;
3. Ensure, monitor and evaluate the progressive implementation of the Kampala Convention (as domesticated);
4. Amend the existing laws of relevant national institutions to accommodate IDPs or enact a separate domestic law on the protection and assistance of IDPs; and
5. Liaise with local and state governments to enact relevant laws on the protection and assistance of IDPs having regard to respective legislative competences under the Nigerian Constitution.

4.3.6 *Funding, monitoring, evaluation, and policy review*

It is significant that the Policy includes this section given as it is crucial to the implementation and improvement of the provisions.[70] As expressed in the sub-heading, this section encompasses funding mechanisms and resource mobilisation, monitoring and evaluation and policy review process. these three sections are considered in turn.

4.3.6.1 *Funding mechanisms and resource mobilisation*

In view of the evident need to ensure that adequate resources are provided to the implementation of the Policy, the inclusion of this section is significant. Notably, this section identifies specific funding sources: (i) joint humanitarian funding mechanisms; (ii) Flash Appeal funding mechanisms; (iii) grants and loans funding mechanisms; and (iv) individual institutional and agency funding mechanisms.

4.3.6.1.1 THE JOINT HUMANITARIAN FUNDING MECHANISM

A joint humanitarian fund (JHF) within the FMHADMSD is contemplated. The proposed structure of this mechanism is clearly expressed in the Policy.

It is contemplated that the FMHADMSD will coordinate an annual Joint Appeal Plan (JAP) which will involve developing a Joint Humanitarian Action Plan (JHAP) premised on the Comprehensive Displacement Management and Implementation Framework (CDMIF). The Policy emphasises that the

> JHAP shall be a joint strategy analysing the political, social and secu-rity situation of the particular situation or crisis; projecting short-term and long-term humanitarian needs; assessing the capacities ofthe agen-cies involved in addressing these needs; and proposing a common set of objectives, actions and indicators for success. A JAP, then, sets out the specific projects and resources required to meet these objectives.

These documents are expected to 'serve as the primary tool to mobilise resources at the field level'.[71] The JHF which will 'serve as a joint donor basket for humanitarian agencies to furnish in preparation for interven-tions'.[72] The Policy further provides that

> intervening donor agencies should be encouraged to contribute a mini-mum of 5% of their resources for intervention into the joint humani-tarian funding basket that shall be deployed on need basis by the FMHADMSD, in consultation with the Inter-Agency Coordination Committee (IACC).[73]

Such contribution is valuable, particularly to the sustenance of humanitar-ian cooperation, however, it would have been pertinent to set out clearly a specific percentage which will be contributed from the government into the JHF. The Policy only mentions that the 'President/Federal Government shall provide seed funds' into the JHF to 'jump-start critical operations, and fund life-saving programmes that are not yet funded'.[74] But in terms of the long-term sustainability of the JHF, it does not categorically provide the percentage funds that will be used for the continuance of the JHF. Such inclusion will have been useful for the purpose of ensuring that the JHF will always have a specific percentage from the government that is constant despite potential changes in donor interventions. priorities and agencies working within the country.

4.3.6.1.2 FLASH APPEAL FUNDING MECHANISM

This is another pertinent mechanism contemplated under the framework for funding. The Policy provides that '[a] shorter Flash Appeal can also be prepared to enable more rapid resource mobilisation and response, although agencies and organisations can also apply for bilateral funding'.[75] This is useful, especially in response to urgent situations or emergencies. However, it would be useful to create a sub-committee within the IACC that is responsible for this appeal in conjunction with the FMHADMSD. This is to ensure urgent deployment, but also create a channel that is predictable and effective to deliver adequate timeous funding.

4.3.6.1.3 GRANTS AND LOANS FUNDING MECHANISMS

This is another stream of funding which is significant in that it reflects on the funding processes beyond the state level. The Policy provides that[76]

> [i]n addition, the Office of the Humanitarian Affairs Coordination of the Presidency could access grants and/or loans available from the UN Central Emergency Response Fund (CERF) and other AU emergency and IDP contingency funding mechanisms to support activities to respond to rapid onset or under-funded emergencies and displacement.

It would also have been useful to specifically include ECOWAS, given that Nigeria is a member of the community.

4.3.6.1.4 INDIVIDUAL INSTITUTIONAL AND AGENCY FUNDING MECHANISMS

The Policy also provides that '[v]arious government and humanitarian agencies shall use their internal funding mechanisms including budgetary allocations to ensure that there are adequate resources for responding to their various sectoral responsibilities in the respective sectors'.[77] This is a significant inclusion that appears to provide a carte-blanche funding stream. However, it would have been useful to specifically also include the private sector given that this sector is already involved in funding IDP protection and assistance.

4.3.6.2 *Monitoring and evaluation*

The Policy emphasises monitoring and evaluation which is crucial to the furtherance of effective implementation of the framework. The Policy provides that '[t]here will be established clear benchmarks for assessing the level of implementation of this policy, and a special monitoring and evaluation unit will be established in the FMHADMSD that shall serve as an IDP databank and clearing house'.[78] Moreover, the Policy reinforces the creation of a National IDP Data Collection and Information System within the

FMHADMSD. This System will be jointly coordinated with the 'Federal Ministry of Communication and Digital Economy'[79] in 'constant consultation with other federal, state and local government agencies as well as CSOs and inter-governmental bodies'.[80] It is significant that this is mentioned given the evident need for data on IDPs.

4.3.6.3 Policy review process

The Policy includes a review process which is useful in order to keep abreast of trends that may arise both normatively and with respect to IDP protection and assistance at various governance levels. Specifically, this section provides that the Policy[81]

> shall be reviewed periodically but not later than five years by the FMHADMSD with a view to making necessary improvements. The review process will be democratic and inclusive and involve wide-range consultations and discussions with all the stakeholders, especially the implementing government agencies, international humanitarian agencies, donor partners, international NGOs, civil society organizations, IDPs and host communities.

A specific inclusion that would have been useful is to give some guidance on the process for review, particularly for predictability, adaptability and in the furtherance of democracy and inclusion.

4.4 Conclusion

While the emergence of the Policy on the landscape of protection and assistance of IDPs in Nigeria is significant, implementation will be of utmost importance if the Policy will significantly actualise the purpose for its formation. As an elaborate framework on IDP protection and assistance, it can serve as the springboard for action by various stakeholders and the evident flexibility of review affords stakeholders the opportunity to test its provisions and revise them in situations where specific actions can be taken for pragmatic outcomes. But the Policy will need to be significantly resourced for effectiveness. And within this context, political will matters. Moreover, the effective coordination by the FMHADMSD in bringing various stakeholders together is needful.

Notes

1 Federal Ministry of Humanitarian Affairs, Disaster Management and Social Development *National Policy on Internally Displaced Persons* (2021).

2 Federal Government of Nigeria *First regional conference on internal displacement in West Africa* (26–28 April 2006), 13 https://www.brookings.edu/wp-content/uploads/2012/04/ECOWAS_rpt_FINAL.pdf (accessed 2 March 2021).

3 Ibid.

4 Federal Republic of Nigeria *National Policy on Internally Displaced Persons in Nigeria* (*Draft*, 2012) 9; The Federal Executive council is the cabinet, and it comprises of the President, the Vice-President and Ministers in charge of various federal government ministries.

5 As above.

6 Samuel Anyanwu 'Ministry of Humanitarian Affairs, FCT Ministry setup Joint Committee on IDPs welfare' *Federal Ministry of Information and Culture (Press Releases)* 10 March 2020 https://fmic.gov.ng/ministry-of-humanitarian-affairs-fct-ministry-setup-joint-committee-on-idps-welfare/ (accessed 6 May 2020).

7 *National Policy on Internally Displaced Persons* (n 1).

8 *National Policy on Internally Displaced Persons* (n 1) 1.

9 *National Policy on Internally Displaced Persons* (n 1) 1.

10 *National Policy on Internally Displaced Persons* (n 1) 2.

11 As above.

12 See Muhammed T Ladan 'Strategies for adopting the National Policy on IDPs and domesticating in Nigeria the African Union Convention for the Protection and Assistance of IDPs in Africa' Paper presented at the National Summit on IDPs in Nigeria, Abuja, Nigeria 19–20 August 2015; Romola Adeola 'The legal protection of internally displaced persons in Nigeria: challenges, imperatives and comparative lessons' in Romola Adeola and Ademola O Jegede *Governance in Nigeria post 1999: revisiting the democratic 'new dawn' of the Fourth Republic* (2019) 222, 226.

13 *National Policy on Internally Displaced Persons* (n 1) 3.

14 As above.

15 As above, 3–4

16 As above, 4.

17 As above.

18 As above.

19 As above.

20 As above, 5–6.

21 As above, 6.

22 As above, 6.

23 These include: arbitrary displacement, armed conflict, armed groups, camps, collective centres, collective shelters, disaster, disaster management, discrimination, durable solutions, early recovery, early warning, emergency, evacuation, forced eviction, Guiding Principles, hazard, host community, humanitarian worker, internal displacement, internally displaced persons, Kampala Convention, livelihoods, missing relative, non-state actors, protection, reintegration, return, returnees, risk, sectors, sexual abuse, sexual exploitation, Sphere Minimum Standards and vulnerability.

24 *National Policy on Internally Displaced Persons* (n 1) 7.

25 As above, 11.

26 As above, 12.

27 As above, 11.

28 As above, 8.

29 As above.

30 As above.

31 As above.
32 As above, 13.
33 As above.
34 As above.
35 As above.
36 As above.
37 As above, 16–18.
38 As above, 18–20.
39 As above, 21.
40 As above, 22.
41 As above.
42 As above.
43 As above, 27.
44 As above, 29.
45 As above, 31.
46 As above.
47 As above, 33.
48 As above, 34–35.
49 As above, 35.
50 As above, 35–36.
51 As above, 36.
52 As above, 38.
53 As above.
54 As above, 40.
55 As above.
56 As above, 42.
57 As above, 44.
58 As above, 49.
59 As above, 53.
60 As above.
61 As above, 54.
62 As above.
63 As above.
64 As above, 55
65 As above, 63–64.
66 As above, 64.
67 As above, 64–65.
68 As above, 66.
69 As above, 67.
70 As above, 68–70.
71 As above, 68.
72 As above.
73 As above.
74 As above.
75 As above, 69.
76 As above.
77 As above.
78 As above.
79 As above, 70.
80 As above.
81 As above.

5 Conclusion

The issue of internal displacement has emerged as a pertinent concern in Nigeria. While much of the discussion on internal displacement in Nigeria has been with respect to the Boko Haram conflict in its north-east region, there have also been other root causes of internal displacement which accentuate the need for a comprehensive approach to the furtherance of protection and assistance of internally displaced persons (IDPs) leveraging the normative frameworks that can provide adequate safeguard. Understanding the legal dimension of protection and assistance is imperative in finding durable solutions to the issue of internal displacement. Within this context, this book is located. This book specifically examines the issue of internal displacement in Nigeria, framing the discussion from a legal perspective.

The Constitution, as the apex law, includes relevant human rights provisions that are applicable to IDPs. There are general frameworks to IDP protection that are relevant, specifically with respect to human rights, humanitarian, migration, environment, refugee, disaster management and land law. However, these provide fragmented responses. Specifically, within the IDP context, there have been attempts towards developing a comprehensive law. In 2021, a National Policy on Internally Displaced Persons (the Policy) was adopted which seeks to set out elaborate protection and assistance for IDPs.[1] While legislation is yet to be adopted, the emergence of the Policy framework is notable, given the numerous attempts at law and policy formations over the last decades.

But having ratified the African Union for the Protection and Assistance of Internally Displaced Persons in Africa (Kampala Convention),[2] I argue that there is an existing state obligation to give effect to the treaty. In giving this effect to it, application in the domestic context is pertinent. It is argued that without prejudice to the requirement of domestication under section 12(1) of the Constitution, the Kampala Convention may be applied in the national context as a supplementary text to the African Charter on Human and Peoples Rights (African Charter),[3] which Nigeria has ratified

DOI: 10.4324/9781003146025-5

and domesticated.[4] This argument is premised on the fact the African Charter establishes supplementary relationships with other instruments that accentuate its provisions. Given that the Kampala Convention establishes human rights protection for IDPs, understanding the human rights corpus with respect to IDPs must be done in connection with the Kampala Convention. Put differently, determining within the national context what the nature of human rights is with respect to IDPs should be construed with reference to the legal text that supplements the African Charter on this issue, i.e., the Kampala Convention. As Nigeria has ratified the Kampala Convention,[5] and as it accepts the provisions of the instrument, an application of the provisions of the Kampala Convention at the domestic level, is without doubt, in line with the inclination of the state on IDP issues.

Overall, it is imperative that a concrete framework on internal displacement be enacted. In this context, it is recommended that a specific national law emerges. For the development of this framework, this chapter proposes certain imperatives integral to the process.

First, it is integral to this process that a *national mapping study* be conducted on existing laws and policies. The aim of this study is to understand the normative landscape across all 36 states and the Federal Capital Territory on issues of internal displacement. This will provide a basis for developing a comprehensive approach and understanding what laws need to be harmonised for the furtherance of a common standard towards the protection and assistance of IDPs. Evidently, the Policy has done some significant groundwork in providing contextual background. However, it is crucial that such mapping examines existing law and policy frameworks across the country.

Second, there must be a *contextual assessment of the dimensions of vulnerability* inherent in the internal displacement situation across the country. The relevance of this contextual assessment is to understand the areas protection needs to be enhanced for IDPs. Moreover, this is imperative in contextualising the law within society and ensuring that it reflects the existing realities of IDPs. In addition to other relevant qualitative methods, this may be done through a survey leveraging on micro-data analysis, particularly at the individual and household level.

Third, there needs to be an *understanding of the protracted situations of internal displacement* and how the law can respond effectively to this issue. As situations of internal displacement may likely be protracted where adequate interventions are not provided, responding to this dimension is integral to advancing durable solutions to IDP concerns.

Fourth, *gender and disability dimensions to internal displacement* must be considered, given the differential impact that internal displacement may have on specific groups. Considering gender is imperative for durable solutions and in order not to treat protection imperatives as a monolith. Such a process will require an evaluation of the experiences of women and girls in displacement to provide evidence-based legal protection. Similarly, it is imperative that a disability-based assessment is also examined in responding to the specific dimensions of protection and assistance of persons with disabilities in the context of internal displacement.

Fifth, it is imperative to address the *institutional dimensions of protection of IDPs* through an analysis of the current state of institutional protection. There are notable institutional approaches to IDP protection reflected in the lead role of the Federal Ministry of Humanitarian Affairs, Disaster Management and Social Development, the activities of agencies such as the National Emergency Management Agency (NEMA) and the National Commission for Refugees, Migrants and IDPs (NCFRMI). In response to the north-east situation, primarily occasioned by the Boko Haram insurgency, a North East Development Commission was established and inaugurated in 2019 with the objective of providing post-conflict reconstruction in the North-East region affected by Boko Haram and fostering socio-economic development in the region.[6] Moreover, given the broad mandate of protecting and promoting human rights, the National Human Rights Commission (NHRC) also engages in IDP protection, co-chairing the Protection Sector Working Group which 'is made up of all organisations government and non-government, national and international working in the protection sector which deals mainly with IDPs, refugees and migrants'.[7] However, there is a need for a more concrete normative grounding of the responsibilities of these institutions. The Policy seeks to provide clarity, but it is crucial for a legislation to establish the mandate of these institutions more firmly with respect to IDPs. This is imperative in order to synergise the activities of institutions working towards IDP protection and ensure that the synergy is reflected in the normative framework. This is also important to determine the required institutional paradigm towards protecting and assisting IDPs in the country.

If protection of IDPs will be a reality within the national context, it is imperative that *political commitment* is reinforced. In building such commitments, advocacy is imperative at various governance levels. This should be sustained through strategic stakeholder sessions within states of the federation. Overall, the legal protection of IDPs must be towards preventing displacement and finding durable solutions in situation where displacement occurs beyond the rhetoric.

Notes

1 Federal Ministry of Humanitarian Affairs, Disaster Management and Social Development *National Policy on Internally Displaced Persons* (2021).
2 African Union Convention for the Protection and Assistance of Internally Displaced Persons in Africa (23 October 2009) (Kampala Convention).

3 African Charter on Human and Peoples' Rights (1981).
4 Nigeria ratified the African Charter on 22 July 1983. See African Union 'List of Countries which have signed, ratified/acceded to the African Charter on Human and Peoples' Rights' (2017).
5 Nigeria ratified the Kampala Convention on 22 May 2012. See African Union 'List of Countries which have signed, ratified/acceded to the African Union Convention for the Protection and Assistance of Internally Displaced Persons in Africa (Kampala Convention)' (2019).
6 Sani Tukur 'Buhari inaugurates board of North East Development Commission' *Premium Times* 8 May 2019; 'The North East Development Commission (NEDC)' *Medium* 8 May 2019.
7 National Human Rights Commission 'Refugees, internally displaced persons, migrants and asylum seekers' https://www.nigeriarights.gov.ng/focus-areas/refugees-internally-displaced-persons-migrants-and-asylum-seekers.html (accessed 2 March 2021).

Bibliography

Books

Abebe, M Allehone *The emerging law on forced migration in Africa: development and implementation of the Kampala Convention on internal displacement* (Routledge, 2016).

Abegunrin, Olayiwola *Nigerian foreign policy under military rule, 1966–1999* (Greenwood Publishing Group Inc, 2003).

Adams, M William *Wasting the rain: rivers, people and planning in Africa* (Earthscan, 1992).

Adeola, Romola *Development-induced displacement and human rights in Africa: the Kampala Convention* (Routledge, 2020).

Adeola, Romola *The internally displaced person in international law* (Edward Elgar, 2020).

Adibe, Jideofor *Nigeria without Nigerians? Boko Haram and the crisis in Nigeria's nation-building project* (Adonis & Abbey Publishers Ltd, 2012).

Adunbi, Omolade *Oil wealth and insurgency in Nigeria* (Indiana University Press, 2015).

Akanle, Olayinka *Kinship networks and international migration in Nigeria* (Cambridge Scholars, 2013).

Anugwom, E Edlyne *The Boko Haram insurgence in Nigeria: perspectives from within* (Palgrave Macmillan, 2019).

Baechler, Günther *Violence through environmental discrimination: causes, Rwanda arena, and conflict model* (Kluwer Academic Publishers, 1999).

Bagshaw, Simon *Developing a normative framework for the protection of internally displaced persons* (Transactional Publishers, 2005).

Bantekas, Ilias and Oette, Lutz *International human rights law and practice* (Cambridge University Press, 2013).

Barnett, Jon and Campbell, John *Climate change and Small Island small states: power, knowledge and the South Pacific* (Earthscan, 2010).

Bellamy, J Alex *The responsibility to protect: a defense* (Oxford University Press, 2015).

Bulkeley, Harriet and Newell, Peter *Governing climate change* (Routledge, 2015).

Cardona-Fox, Gabriel *Exile within borders: a global look at commitment to the international regime to protect internally displaced persons* (Brill, 2019).

Cantor, J David *Returns of internally displaced persons during armed conflict: international law and its application in Columbia* (Brill-Nijhoff, 2018).

Cohen, Roberta and Deng, M Francis *Masses in flight: the global crisis of internal displacement* (Brookings Institution Press, 1998).

Cohen, Roberta and Deng, M Francis (eds) *The forsaken people: case studies of the internally displaced* (Brookings Institution, 1998).

Cullen, Anthony *The concept of non-international armed conflict in international humanitarian law* (Cambridge University Press, 2010).

David, J Ojochenemi, Asuelime, E Lucky and Onapajo, Hakeem *Boko Haram: the socio-economic drivers* (Springer, 2015).

de Schutter, Olivier *International human rights law: cases, materials, commentary* (Cambridge University Press, 2010).

Donato, M Katharine and Gabaccia, Donna *Gender and international migration: from the slavery era to the global age* (Russell Sage Foundation, 2015).

Donnelly, Jack *Universal human rights in theory and practice* (Cornell University Press, 2013).

Dinstein, Yoram *Non-international armed conflicts in international law* (Cambridge University Press, 2014).

Ekhomu, Ona *Boko Haram: security considerations and the rise of an insurgency* (CRC Press, 2020)

Falola, Toyin and Ihonvbere, O Julius *The rise and fall of Nigeria's Second Republic: 1979–1984* (Zed Books, 1985).

Faluyi, T Olumuyiwa, Khan, Sultan and Akinola, O Adeoye *Boko Haram's terrorism and the Nigerian state: federalism, politics and policies* (Springer, 2019).

Forrest, Tom *Politics and economic development in Nigeria: updated edited* (Avalon Publishing, 1995).

Forsyth, Frederick *The Biafra story: the making of an African legend* (Pen & Sword Books Ltd, 2015).

Gibney, Mark *International human rights law: returning to universal principles* (Rowman & Littlefield Publishers Inc, 2008).

Grahl-Madsen, Atle *The status of refugees in international law: refugee character* (AW Sijthoff, 1966).

Hampton, Janie *Internally displaced people: a global survey* (Earthscan, 2002).

Ibhawoh, Bonny *Human rights in Africa* (Cambridge University Press, 2018).

Kaigama, A Ignatius *Peace, not war: a decade of interventions in the Plateau state crises (2001–2011)* (Hamtul Press Ltd, 2012).

Kälin, Walter and Künzli, Jörg *The law of international human rights protection* (Oxford University Press, 2009).

Kendhammer, Brandon and McCain, Carmen *Boko Haram* (Ohio University Press, 2018).

Korn, A David *Exodus within borders: an introduction to the crisis of internal displacement* (The Brookings Institution 1999).

Kufuor, O Kofi *The African human rights system: origin and evolution* (Palgrave Macmillan, 2010).

Kuwali, Dan *The responsibility to protect: implementation of article 4(h) intervention* (Martinus Nijhoff, 2011).

Kuwali, Dan and Viljoen, Frans (eds) *Africa and the responsibility to protect: article 4(h) of the African Union Constitutive Act* (Routledge, 2014).

Leroux, Marcel *Global warming – myth or reality? The erring ways of climatology* (Springer, 2006).

Marks, Susan and Clapham, Andrew *International human rights lexicon* (Oxford University Press, 2005).

Maru, T Mehari *The Kampala Convention and its contribution to international law: legal analyses and interpretations of the African Union Convention for the protection and assistance of internally displaced persons* (Eleven Publishing, 2014).

Maszka, John *Al-Shabaab and Boko Haram: guerrilla insurgency or strategic terrorism?* (World Scientific Publishing Europe Ltd, 2018).

Murray, Rachel *The African Charter on human and peoples' rights: a commentary* (Oxford University Press, 2019).

Obilade, O Akintunde *The Nigerian legal system* (Sweet and Maxwell, 1979).

Okafo, Nonso *Reconstructing law and justice in a postcolony* (Routledge, 2016).

Okoli, SA Chukwuma and Oppong, F Richard *Private international law in Nigeria* (Hart Publishing, 2020).

Okonta, Ike and Douglas, Oronto *Where vultures feast: Shell, human rights, and oil in the Niger Delta* (Verso, 2003).

Olawuyi, S Damilola *The human rights-based approach to carbon finance* (Cambridge University Press, 2016).

Omeni, Akali *Insurgency and war in Nigeria: regional fracture and the fight against Boko Haram* (Bloomsburg Publishing, 2020).

Ouguergouz, Fatsah *African Charter on human and peoples' rights: a comprehensive agenda for human dignity and sustainable democracy in Africa* (Martinus Nijhoff Publishers, 2003).

Peel, Michael *A swamp full of dollars: pipelines and paramilitaries at Nigeria's oil frontier* (Bloomsbury Publishing, 2009).

Pittock, A Barrie *Climate change: the science, impacts and solutions* (Earthscan, 2009).

Phuong, Catherine *The international protection of internally displaced persons* (Cambridge University Press, 2004).

Romanova, Irina *Oil boom in Nigeria and its consequences for the country's economic development* (GRIN Verlag, 2007).

Ssenyonjo, Manisuli *Economic, social and cultural rights in international law* (Hart Publishing, 2016).

Shelton, Dinah *Remedies in international human rights law* (Oxford University Press, 2015).

Shelton, L Dinah *Advanced introduction to international human rights law* (Edward Elgar Publishing Limited, 2014).

Sivakumaran, Sandesh *The law of non-international armed conflict* (Oxford University Press, 2012).

Smith, KM Rhona *International human rights law* (Oxford University Press, 2018).

Solomon, Hussein *Terrorism and counter-terrorism in Africa: fighting insurgency from Al Shabaab, Ansar Dine and Boko Haram* (Springer, 2015).

Sundiata, K Ibrahim *Equatorial Guinea: Colonialism, state terror, and the search for stability* (Routledge, 1990).

Swindell, Ken *Farm labour* (Cambridge University Press, 1985).

Thurston, Alexander *Boko Haram: the history of an African jihadist movement* (Princeton University Press, 2018).

Tomuschat, Christian *Human rights: between idealism and realism* (Oxford University Press, 2014).

Umozurike, U Oji *The African Charter on human and peoples' rights* (Martinus Nijhoff, 1997).

Uwakah, T Onyebuchi *Due process in Nigeria's administrative law system: history, current status and future* (University Press of America, 1997).

Uzokwe, O Alfred *Surviving in Biafra: the story of the Nigerian civil war: over two million died* (iUniverse, 2003).

Varin, Caroline *Boko Haram and the war on terror* (ABC-CLIO, LLC, 2016).

Viljoen, Frans *International human rights law in Africa* (Oxford University Press, 2012).

Walker, Andrew *'Eat the heart of the infidel': the harrowing of Nigeria and the rise of Boko Haram* (C Hurst & Co (Publishers) Ltd, 2016).

Wangbu, K John *The Niger Delta paradox: impoverished in the midst of abundance* (Safari Books Ltd, 2018).

Weiss, G Thomas and Korn, A David *Internal displacement: conceptualization and its consequences* (Routledge, 2006).

Whelan, J Daniel *Indivisible human rights: a history* (University of Pennsylvania Press, 2010).

Wolf, Sonja *Mano dura: the politics of gang control in El Salvador* (University of Texas Press, 2017).

Chapters in books

Adeola, Romola 'Protecting climate change induced internally displaced persons in Africa: relevance of the Kampala Convention' in Filho L Walter (ed) *Handbook of climate change resilience* (Springer, 2019).

Adeola, Romola 'The legal protection of internally displaced persons in Nigeria: challenges, imperatives and comparative lessons' in Romola Adeola and Ademola O Jegede (eds) *Governance in Nigeria post 1999: revisiting the democratic 'new dawn' of the Fourth Republic* (Pretoria University Law Press, 2019).

Aghedo, Iro 'Old wine in a new bottle: ideological and operational linkages between Maitatsine and Boko Haram revolts in Nigeria' in James J Hentz and Hussein Solomon (eds) *Understanding Boko Haram: terrorism and insurgency in Africa* (Routledge, 2017).

Ajibewa, Aderemi 'The Third Republic and Nigeria's foreign policy options' in Bamidele A Ojo (ed) *Third Republic: the problems and prospects of political transition to civil rule* (Nova Science Publishers Inc, 1998).

Anyalemechi, O Godwin 'Terrorism and cross-border insurgency as new threats and challenges to peace and security in Africa: the Boko Haram insurgency' in

Iyi John-Mark and Strydom Hennie (eds) *Boko Haram and international law* (Springer, 2018).

Chirwa, M Danwood 'The Universal Declaration of Human Rights, economic, social and cultural rights and human rights discourse' in Ferstman Carla, Goldberg Alexander, Gray Tony, Ison Liz, Nathan Richard and Newman Michael (eds) *Contemporary human rights challenges: the Universal Declaration of Human Rights and its continuing relevance* (Routledge, 2019).

David, Eric 'Internal (non-international) armed conflict' in Andrew Clapham and Paola Gaeta (eds) *The Oxford handbook of international law in armed conflict* (Oxford University Press, 2014).

Dietz, Ton 'Ecospace, humanspace and climate change' in Salih MA Mohamed (ed) *Climate change and sustainable development: new challenges for poverty reduction* (Edward Elgar Publishing, 2009).

Duchatellier, Moetsi and Phuong, Catherine 'The African contribution to the protection of internally displaced persons: a commentary on the 2009 Kampala Convention' in Vincent Chetail and Céline Bauloz (eds) *Research handbook on international law and migration* (Edward Elgar, 2014).

Filho, L Walter, Tetteh, K Isaac and Musa, M Haruna 'Trends in climate change in Africa' in Thomas-Hope Elizabeth (eds) *Climate change and food security: Africa and the Caribbean* (Routledge, 2018).

Halliru, L Salisu and Umar, A Da'u 'Climate change and rural water supply planning in Nigeria' in Filho L Walter (ed) *Climate change and the sustainable use of water resources* (Springer, 2012).

Jegede, O Ademola 'Indigenous peoples, climate migration and international human rights law in Africa, with reflections on the relevance of the Kampala Convention' in Mayer Benoît and Crépeau François (eds) *Research handbook on climate change, migration and the law* (Edward Elgar, 2017).

Kälin, Walter 'Conceptualising climate-induced displacement' in Jane McAdam (ed) *Climate change and displacement: multidisciplinary perspectives* (Hart Publishing, 2010).

Khajuria, Sanjay 'Water, climate change and sustainable development' in Biswas K Asit and Tortajada Cecilia (eds) *Water security, climate change and sustainable development* (Springer, 2016).

Maxted, Julia 'Exploitation of energy resources in Africa' in Sernau R Scott (ed) *Contemporary readings in globalization* (Sage Publications Inc, 2008).

Nwanna, Chinwe 'Governance and local government elections in Nigeria's Fourth Republic' in Osita Agbu (ed) *Elections and governance in Nigeria's Fourth Republic* (Council for the Development of Social Science Research in Africa, 2016).

Ranum, C Elin 'Street gangs in Guatemala' in Thomas Bruneau, Lucía Damme and Elizabeth Skinner (eds) *Maras: gang violence and security in Central America* (University of Texas Press, 2011).

Reder, Michael 'Climate change and human rights' in Edenhofer Ottmar, Wallacher Johannes, Lotze-Campen Hermann, Reder Michael, Knopf Brigitte and Müller Johannes (eds) *Climate change, justice and sustainability: linking climate and development policy* (Springer, 2012).

Selvaraju, Ramasamy 'Implications of climate change for agriculture and food security in the western Asia and northern Africa region' in Sivakumar VK Mannava, Selvaraju LR Rattan and Ibrahim Hamdan (eds) *Climate change and food security in West Asia and North Africa* (Springer, 2013).

Umukoro, G Francis 'Politicisation and underdevelopment of the Niger Delta region' in Ojakorotu Victor (ed) *Anatomy of the Niger Delta crisis: causes, consequences and opportunities for peace* (LIT Verlag, 2010).

Viljoen, Frans 'Africa's contribution to the development of international human rights and humanitarian law' in Sahle N Eunice (ed) *Human rights in Africa contemporary debates and struggles* (Palgrave Macmillan, 2019).

Journal articles

Aboda, Caroline, Mugagga, Frank, Byakagaba, Patrick and Nabanoga, Goretti 'Development induced displacement: a review of risks faced by communities in developing countries' (2019) 7(2) *Sociology and Anthropology* 100.

Adeola, Romola 'The legal protection of development-induced displaced persons in Africa' (2017) 10(1) *African Journal of Legal Studies* 91.

Adeola, Romola 'Xenophobia and internal displacement in Africa: defining protection and assistance through the Kampala Convention' (2020) 27(4) *South African Journal of International Affairs* 493.

Adeola, Romola, Viljoen, Frans and Muhindo, M Trésor 'A commentary on the African Commission's general comment on the Right to Freedom of Movement and Residence under article 12(1) of the African Charter on human and peoples' rights' (2021) *Journal of African Law* 1–21.

Adigun, Muyiwa 'The implementation of the African Charter on Human and Peoples' rights and the Convention on the rights of the child in Nigeria: the creation of irresponsible parents and dutiful children?' (2019) 51 *The Journal of Legal Pluralism and Unofficial Law* 320.

Adigun, Muyiwa 'The status of customary international law under the Nigerian legal system' (2019) 45(1) *Commonwealth Law Bulletin* 115.

Agbaje, BA Elijah 'Modernisation, urban renewal and the social cost of development' (2013) 4(10) *Mediterranean Journal of Social Sciences* 318.

Agbiboa, E Daniel 'Why Boko Haram exists: the relative deprivation perspective' (2013) 3(1) *African Conflict and Peacebuilding Review* 144.

Agbonifo, John 'Oil, insecurity, and subversive patriots in the Niger Delta: the Ogoni as agent of revolutionary change' (2009) 26(2) *Journal of Third World Studies* 71.

Ako, Rhuks 'The struggle for resource control and violence in the Niger Delta' in Obi Cyril and Rustad A Siri (eds) *Oil and insurgency in the Niger Delta: managing the complex politics of petro-violence* (Zed Books, 2011).

Albert, O Isaac 'Electoral violence in the Nigerian "Fourth Republic": the paradox of democracy' (2011) 3(239) *Afrique Contemporaine* 105.

Ambe-Uva, N Terhemba 'Identity politics and the Jos crisis: evidence, lessons and challenges of good governance' (2010) 2(3) *African Journal of History and Culture* 42.

Angerbrandt, Henrik 'Political decentralisation and conflict: the Sharia crisis in Kaduna, Nigeria' (2011) 29(1) *Journal of Contemporary African Studies* 15.

Angerbrandt, Henrik 'Religion, ethnicity and citizenship: demands for territorial self-determination in southern Kaduna, Nigeria' (2014) 33(2) *Journal of Contemporary African Studies* 232.

Albert, O Isaac 'Rethinking the functionality of the Multinational Joint Task Force in managing the Boko Haram crisis in the Lake Chad Basin' (2017) 42(3) *Africa Development* 119.

Alfaro-Velcamp, Theresa and Shaw, Mark '"Please go home and build Africa": criminalizing immigrants in South Africa' (2016) 42(5) *Journal of Southern African Studies* 983.

Aluko, Olajide 'The expulsion of illegal aliens from Nigeria: a study in Nigeria's decision-making' (1985) 84(337) *African Affairs* 539.

Aworawo, David 'Decisive thaw: the changing pattern of relations between Nigeria and Equatorial Guinea, 1980–2005' (2010) 1 *Journal of International and Global Studies* 89.

Badmus, A Isiaka 'Oiling the guns and gunning for oil: oil violence, arms proliferation and the destruction of Nigeria's Niger-Delta' (2010) 2(1) *Journal of Alternative Perspectives in the Social Sciences* 323.

Bailey, C Leslie 'Out of Africa: toward regional solutions for internal displacement' (2014) 39(1) *Brooklyn Journal of International Law* 353.

Cantor, J David 'As deadly as armed conflict? Gang violence and forced displacement in the Northern Triangle of Central America' (2016) 23(34) *Agenda Internacional* 77.

Deng, Francis 'International response to internal displacement: a revolution in the making' (2004) 11(3) *Human Rights Brief* 1.

de Moraes Farais, F Paolo 'A letter from Ki-Toro Mahamman Gaani, King of Busa (Borgu, Northern Nigeria) about the "Kisra" stories of origin (c. 1910)' (1992) 3 *Sudanic Africa* 109.

Dieng, Adama 'Protecting internally displaced: the value of the Kampala Convention as a regional example' (2017) 99(904) *International Review of the Red Cross* 263.

D'Orsi, Cristiano 'Strengths and weaknesses in the protection of the internally displaced persons in Sub-Saharan Africa' (2012) 28(1) *Connecticut Journal of International Law* 73.

Dinslage, Sabine and Leger, Rudolf 'Language and migration the impact of the Jukun on Chadic speaking groups in the Benue-Gongola basin' (1996) 268(8) *Berichte des Sonderforschungsbereichs* 67.

Dze-Ngwa, Willibroad 'The Multinational Joint Task Force against Boko Haram: rethinking military interventions' (2018) 6(7) *International Journal of Liberal Arts and Social Science* 15.

Ekhator, O Eghosa 'The impact of the African Charter on Human and Peoples' Rights on domestic law: a case study of Nigeria' (2015) 41(2) *Commonwealth Law Bulletin* 253.

Ezeanokwasa, O Jude, Kalu, C Uwadineke and Okaphor, E Francis 'A critique of the legal framework for arresting the threat of internal displacement of persons to Nigeria's national security' (2018) 9(2) *Nnamdi Azikiwe University Journal of International Law and Jurisprudence* 10.

Ferris, Elizabeth 'Assessing the impact of the principles: an unfinished task' (2008) 10 *Forced Migration Review* 10–11.

Ferris, Elizabeth 'Internal displacement and the right to seek asylum' (2008) 27(3) *Refugee Survey Quarterly* 76.

Füssel, Hans-Martin and Klein, JT Richard 'Climate change vulnerability assessments: an evolution of conceptual thinking' (2006) 75 *Climate Change* 301.

Giorgi, Filippo and Lionello, Piero 'Climate change projections for the Mediterranean region' (2008) 63(2/3) *Global and Planetary Change* 90.

Goldman, K Robert 'Internal displacement, the guiding principles on internal displacement, the principles normative status, and the need for their effective domestic implementation in Colombia' (2009) 2 *Anuario Colombiano de Derecho Internacional* 59.

Groth, Lauren 'Engendering protection: an analysis of the 2009 Kampala Convention and its provision for internally displaced women' (2011) 23(2) *International Journal of Refugee Law* 221.

Guistiniani, Z Flavia 'New hopes and challenges for the protection of IDPs in Africa: the Kampala Convention for the protection and assistance of internally displaced persons in Africa' (2011) 39(2) *Denver Journal of International Law and Policy* 347.

Henckaerts, Jean-Marie 'Study on customary international humanitarian law: a contribution to the understanding and respect for the rule of law in armed conflict' (2005) 87(857) *International Review of the Red Cross* 175.

Juma, Laurence 'The narrative of vulnerability and deprivation in protection regimes for the internally displaced persons (IDPs) in Africa: an appraisal of the Kampala Convention' (2012) 16 *Law, Democracy and Development* 219.

Kamungi, Prisca 'Beyond good intentions: implementing the Kampala Convention' (2010) 34 *Forced Migration Review* 53.

Kazah-Toure, Toure 'The political economy of ethnic conflicts and governance in southern Kaduna, Nigeria: [de]constructing a contested terrain' (1999) 24(1) *Africa Development* 109.

Keohane, O Robert and Victor, G David 'The regime complex for climate change' (2011) 9(1) *Perspectives on Politics* 7.

Kutigi, D Halima 'Towards justiciability of economic, social and cultural rights in Nigeria: a role for Canadian-Nigerian cooperation?' (2017) 4 *The Transnational Human Rights Review* 125.

Kuwali, Dan 'From durable solutions to holistic solutions: prevention of displacement in Africa' (2014) 6(2/3) *African Journal of Legal Studies* 265.

Loarie, R Scott, Duffy, B Philip, Hamilton, Healy, Asner, P Gregory, Field, B Christopher and Ackerly, D David 'The velocity of climate change' (2009) 462 *Nature* 1052.

Madueke, L Kingsley 'From neighbours to deadly enemies: excavating landscapes of territoriality and ethnic violence in Jos, Nigeria' (2018) 36(1) *Journal of Contemporary African Studies* 87.

Maru, T Mehari 'The Kampala Convention and its contribution in filling the protection gap in international law' (2011) 1(1) *Journal of Internal Displacement* 91.

Merhof, Katrin 'Building a bridge between reality and the Constitution: the establishment and development of the Columbia Constitutional Court' (2015) 13(3) *International Journal of Constitutional Law* 714.

Mmom, C Prince and Igwe, F Chimezie 'Environmental degradation resulting from oil exploitation, and population displacement in the Niger Delta, Nigeria' (2012) 1 *Journal of Environmental Science and Engineering* 125.

Nnadi, O Godwin, Ezeani, Emmanuel Onyebuchi and Nnadi, H Chinedu 'The National Emergency Management Agency (NEMA) and the challenge of effective management of internally displaced persons in North Eastern Nigeria' (2020) 25(5) *IOSR Journal of Humanities and Social Science* 14.

Nwafor, O Anthony 'Enforcing fundamental rights in Nigerian courts – processes and challenges' (2009) 4 *African Journal of Legal Studies* 1.

Obamamoye, F Babatunde 'Counter-terrorism, Multinational Joint Task Force and the missing components' (2017) 15(4) *African Identities* 428.

Obiadi, N Bons, Onochie, O Aloysius and Uduak, U Peter 'Where is home for the Abuja, Nigeria urban poor' (2019) 8(1) *Mgbakoigba, Journal of African Studies* 50.

Obi, Cyril 'Nigeria's Niger Delta: understanding the complex drivers of violent oil-related conflict' (2009) 34(2) *Africa Development* 103.

Ogunrinde, A Temitope, Oguntunde, G Philip, Akinwumiju, S Akinola, Fasinmirin, T Johnson 'Analysis of recent changes in rainfall and drought indices in Nigeria, 1981–2015' (2019) 64(14) *Hydrological Sciences Journal* 1755.

Okebukola, O Elijah 'The application of international law in Nigeria and the façade of dualism' (2020) 11(1) *Nnamdi Azikwe University Journal of International Law and Jurisprudence* 15.

Ojeda, Stephanie 'The Kampala Convention on internally displaced persons: some international humanitarian law aspects' (2010) 29(3) *Refugee Survey Quarterly* 58.

Ojukwu, N Chudi 'Enforcement of the African Charter on human and peoples' rights as a domestic law in Nigeria' (2000) 25(4) *International Legal Practitioner* 140.

Olawepo, A Raphael 'Resettlement and agricultural change in a rural Nigerian environment: the Jebba scheme example' (2006) 2(1) *International Journal of Rural Management* 57.

Onapajo, Hakeem, Uzodike, O Ufo and Whetho, Ayo 'Boko Haram terrorism in Nigeria: the international dimension' (2012) 19(3) *South African Journal of International Affairs* 337.

Onyemelukwe, Cheluchi 'Legislating on violence against women: a critical analysis of Nigeria's recent Violence Against Persons (Prohibition) Act, 2015' (2016) 5(2) *DePaul Journal of Women, Gender and the Law* 1.

Opukri, O Christian and Ibaba, S Ibaba 'Oil induced environmental degradation and internal population displacement in the Nigeria's Niger Delta' (2008) 10(1) *Journal of Sustainable Development in Africa* 173.

Orchid, Phil 'Protection of internally displaced persons: soft law as a norm generating mechanism' (2010) 36(2) *Review of International Studies* 281.

Oruonye, D Emeka 'An assessment of the socio-economic impact of urban development-induced resettlement scheme in Nigerian cities: a case study of the Nyamusala – ATC road construction in Jalingo Metropolis, Taraba state' (2012) 3(1) *International Review of Social Sciences and Humanities* 1.

Oyefara, L John and Alabi, O Bamidele 'Socio-economic consequences of development-induced internal displacement and the coping strategies of female victims in Lagos, Nigeria: an ethno-demographic study' (2016) 30(2) *African Population Studies* 2520.

Parmesan, Camille and Yohe, Gary 'A globally coherent fingerprint of climate change impacts across natural systems' (2003) 421 *Nature* 37.

Peil, Margaret 'The expulsion of West African aliens' (1971) 9(2) *The Journal of Modern African Studies* 205.

Ridderbos, Katinka 'The Kampala Convention and obligations of armed groups' (2011) 37 *Forced Migration Review* 36.

Rodríguez-Garavito, César 'Beyond the courtroom: the impact of judicial activism on socioeconomic rights in Latin America' (2011) 89 *Texas Law Review* 1669.

Sanni, Abiola 'Fundamental rights enforcement procedure rules, 2009 as a tool for the enforcement of the African Charter on human and peoples' rights in Nigeria: the need for far-reaching reform' (2011) 11 *African Human Rights Law Journal* 511.

Stavropoulou, Maria 'The Kampala Convention and protection from arbitrary displacement' (2010) 36 *Forced Migration Review* 62.

Tar, A Usman and Sunday, Adejoh 'Military alliance and counter-terrorism in sub-Saharan Africa: the Multi-national Joint Task Force in perspective' (2017) 5(2) *Covenant University Journal of Politics and International Affairs* 1.

Tesfaye, Amare 'Internally displaced persons in Africa: a glimpse view of the protections accorded in the Kampala Convention' (2017) 9 *Jimma University Journal of Law* 1.

Viljoen, Frans 'Application of the African Charter on human and peoples' rights by domestic courts in Africa' (1999) 43(1) *Journal of African Law* 1.

Waddington, Conway 'In the fight against Boko Haram, the Multinational Joint Task Force limps forward' (2015) 7 *Africa Conflict Monitor* 50.

Walker, H Julian, Lipietz, Barbara, Ohaeri, Victoria, Onyebueke, Victor and Ujah, Oliver 'Displacement and the public interest in Nigeria: contesting developmental rationales for displacement' (2019) *Development in Practice* 1.

Wallace, Tina 'Agricultural projects and land in northern Nigeria' (1980) 17 *Review of African Political Economy* 59.

Yntiso, Gebre 'Urban development and displacement in Addis Ababa: the impact of resettlement projects on low income households' (2008) 24(2) *Eastern Africa Social Science Research Review* 53.

Resolutions, treaties, guidelines, principles, and policy instruments

African Charter on Human and Peoples' Rights (1981).
African Charter on Human and Peoples' Rights (Ratification and Enforcement) Act (1983).
African Charter on the Rights and Welfare of the Child (1990).
African Union Convention for the Protection and Assistance of Internally Displaced Persons in Africa (23 October 2009).
Child's Rights Act (2003).
Convention on the Rights of the Child (1989).
Environmental Impact Assessment Act (1992).
General Comment No 5 on the African Charter on Human and Peoples' Rights: The Right to Freedom of Movement and Residence (article 12(1)) (2019).
Geneva Convention for the Amelioration of the Condition of the Wounded and Sick in Armed Forces in the Field (12 August 1949).
Geneva Convention for the Amelioration of the Condition of Wounded, Sick and Shipwrecked Members of Armed Forces at Sea (12 August 1949).
Geneva Convention Relative to the Treatment of Prisoners of War (12 August 1949).
Geneva Convention Relative to the Protection of Civilian Persons in Time of War (12 August 1949).
Global Compact on Safe, Orderly and Regular Migration (2018).
Immigration Act (1963).
International Covenant on Economic, Social and Cultural Rights, adopted by the UN General Assembly Resolution 2200A (XXI), UN Doc A/6316 (16 December 1966).
International Covenant on Civil and Political Rights, adopted by the UN General Assembly Resolution 2200A (XXI), UN Doc A/6316 (16 December 1966).
Land Use Act (1978).
Montevideo Convention on the Rights and Duties of States (1933).
National Commission for Refugees (Establishment, Etc.) Act 2004.
National Environmental Standards and Regulations Enforcement Act (2007).
National Migration Policy (2015).
OAU Refugee Convention Governing the Specific Aspects of Refugee Problems in Africa (1969).
Oil Pipelines Act (1956).
Petroleum Act (1969).
Protocol Additional to the Geneva Conventions of 12 August 1949 and Relating to the Protection of Victims of International Armed Conflict (8 June 1977).

Protocol Additional to the Geneva Conventions of 12 August 1949 and Relating to the Protection of Victims of Non-international Armed Conflict (Additional Protocol II) (8 June 1977).

Protocol on the Protection and Assistance to Internally Displaced Persons, adopted by International Conference on the Great Lakes (30 November 2006).

Protocol Relating to the Status of Refugees (1967).

Protocol to the African Charter on Human and Peoples' Rights on the Rights of Older Persons (2016).

Protocol to the African Charter on Human and Peoples' Rights on the Rights of Persons with Disabilities in Africa (2018).

Protocol to the African Charter on Human and Peoples' Rights on the Rights of Women in Africa (2003).

Rome Statute of the International Criminal Court (1998).

The Revised Migration Policy Framework for Africa and Plan of Action (2018–2027).

Universal Declaration of Human Rights, adopted by the UN General Assembly Resolution 217 A (III) of 10 December 1948

United Nations Guiding Principles on Internal Displacement (1998).

United Nations Refugee Convention Relating to the Status of Refugees (1951).

Vienna Convention on the Law of Treaties 1969 1155 UNTS 331.

Cases

Abacha v Fawehinmi (2000) LPELR-14 (SC).

Adamu & Ors v. Attorney General of Borno State (1998) 8 NWLR 203.

Adedeji & Sons Motors Nigeria Limited v Immeh & Anor LPELR-14104 (CA) (1996).

Adetoun Oladeji (Nig) Ltd v Nigerian Breweries Plc LPELR-160 (SC) (2007).

Agbaje v Fashola (2008) 6 NWLR (Pt 1082).

Agemo & Others v Attorney General of Lagos State & Ors Suit No. LD/4232MFHR/16 (2017).

Alhaji Wahabi Layiwola Olatunji v The Military Governor of Oyo state & Ors (1994) LPELR-14116 (CA).

Ambo Wuyah v Jama'a Local Government, Kafanchan (2011) LPELR-9078 (CA).

Amos & Ors (for themselves as individual and on behalf of Ogbia Community Brass Division) v Shell B.P Petroleum Development Company of Nigeria Limited and Anor (1977) 6 SC 109.

Aqua v Archibong & Ors (2012) LPELR-9293(CA).

Aso Tim Doz Investment Company Limited v Abuja Markets Management Limited & Anor (2016) LPELR-40367 (CA).

Attorney General of the Federation v Attorney General of Lagos State LPELR-20974 (SC) (2013).

Centre for Oil Pollution Watch v Nigeria National Petroleum Corporation (2019) 5 NWLR (Pt 1666) 518.

Chinda & 5 Others v Shell-BP Petroleum Development Company of Nigeria Limited (1974) 2 RSLR 1.

Columbia Constitutional Court, Decision T-025 of 2004.

Communication 155/96: *Social and Economic Rights Action Center (SERAC) and Center for Economic and Social Rights (CESR) v Nigeria.*

C.S.S Bookshop Ltd v Registered Trustees of Muslim Community in River States & Ors (2006) LPELR-SC.307/2001.

Dada v State (1977) NCLR 135.

Douglas v Shell Petroleum Development Company Nigeria Limited (1999) 2 NWLR (Part 591) 466.

ELF Nigeria Ltd v Sillo & Anor (For themselves and on behalf of Sillo family of Obodo) (1994) 6 NWLR (Part 350) 258.

Goldmark Nigeria Limited & Ors v Ibafon Company Limited & Ors (2012) LPELR-SC 421/2001.

Ikpede v The Shell BP Petroleum Development Company Nigeria Limited (1973) MWSJ 61.

Kalu v Odili & Ors LPELR-1653 (SC) (1992).

Kandix Ltd & Anor v AG & Commissioner for Justice, Cross River State & Anor (2010) LPELR-4389 (CA).

Lafia Local Govt v Executive Govt, Nasarawa State & Ors (2012) LPELR-20602 (SC).

Master v Mansur & Ors LPELR-23440 (CA) (2014).

Medical and Dental Practitioners Disciplinary tribunal v Okonkwo (2001) LPELP-1856 (SC).

Mon & Anor v Shell Petroleum Development Company Nigeria Limited (1973) 1 RSLR 71.

Mrs Georgina Ahamefule v Imperial Medical Centre & Dr Alex K Molokwu Suit No. ID/1627/2000 (2012).

Mustapha v Governor of Lagos State & Ors (1987) LPELR-1931 (SC).

Nigeria Arab Bank Ltd v Barri Engineering Nig Ltd LPELR-2007 (SC) (1995).

Njoku & Ors v Iheanatu & Ors CA/PH/EPT/454/2007 (2008).

Nsirim v Nsirim LPELR-8060 (SC) (2002).

Nwadiaro & 2 Others v Shell Petroleum Development Company Nigeria Limited (1990) 5 NWLR. (Part 150) 322.

Nwali & Ebsiec & Ors (2014) LPELR-23682 (CA).

Odafe & Another v Attorney-General & Others (2004) AHRLR 205 (NgHC 2004).

Ogiale v Shell Petroleum Development Company Nigeria Limited (1997) 1 NWLR (Pt. 480) 148.

Ojukwu v Agupusi & Anor LPELR-22683 (CA) (2014).

Ojukwu v Military Governor of Lagos State & Ors CA/L/196/85 (1) (1985).

Okafor & Ors v Ntoka & Ors (2017) LPELR-42794 (CA).

Okafor v Lagos State Govt and Anor (2016) LPELR-41066 (CA).

Okogie v Attorney-General of Lagos State (1981) 1 NCLR 218.

Omega Bank Plc v Government of Ekiti State (2007) All FWLR (Pt. 386) 658.

Oni v Fayemi NWLR (Pt 1089) 400 at 427–428 (2008).

Oseku v The Minister FCT, Abuja & Ors LPELR-3560 (CA) (2007).

Oyewunmi & Anor v Ogunesan LPELR-2880 (SC) (1990).

Pfizer Specialities Ltd v Chyzob Pharmacy Ltd (2008) All FWLR (Pt. 414) 1455.

Rhodes & Anor v IGP & Ors (2018) LPELR-44118 (CA).

Sheka v Bashari LPELR-21403 (CA) (2013).

Shell Petroleum Development Company Nigeria Ltd v Amaro & Ors (2000) 10 NWLR (Part 675) 248.

Shell Petroleum Development Company of Nigeria Limited v Ambah (1991) 3 NWLR (Part 593) 1.

Shell Petroleum Development Company Nigeria Limited v Edamkue & Others (2009) 10 SCM 150.

Shell Petroleum Development Company of Nigeria Limited v Enoch & 2 Ors (1992) 8 NWLR (Part 259) 335.

Shell Petroleum Development Company Nigeria Limited v Farah & 7 Others (1995) 3 NWLR. (Part 382) 148.

Shell Petroleum Development Company Nigeria Limited v Isaiah (2001) 11 N.W.L.R. (Part 723) 168.

Shell Petroleum Development Company Nigeria Ltd v Otoko (1996) 6 NWLR (Part 150) 639.

Shell Petroleum Development Company, Nigeria Ltd v Tiebo VII & Others (2005) 3–4 S.C.

Shell Petroleum Development Company Nigeria Limited v Udi (1996) 6 NWLR (Part 455) 483.

Shell Petroleum Development Company of Nigeria Limited v Uzoaru & 3 Ors (For themselves and as representing the Umunnaka Ukwu village of Oguta) (1994) 9 NWLR (Part 366) 51.

The Prosecutor v Duško Tadić International Criminal Tribunal of the Former Yugoslavia, Appeals Chamber (IT-94-1-AR72) (2 October 1995).

The Prosecutor v Jean Paul Akayesu International Criminal Tribunal for Rwanda, Trial Chamber 1 (ICTR-96-4-T) (2 September 1998).

The Prosecutor v Jean-Pierre Bemba Gombo International Criminal Court, Trial Chamber III (ICC-01/05-01/08) (21 March 2016).

The Prosecutor v Jean-Pierre Bemba Gombo International Criminal Court, The Appeals Chamber (ICC-01/05-01/08) (8 June 2018).

The Prosecutor v Jean-Pierre Bemba Gombo International Criminal Court, The Appeals Chamber (ICC-01/05-01/08) (14 June 2018) (Concurring Separate Opinion of Judge Eboe-Osuji) https://www.icc-cpi.int/RelatedRecords/CR2018 _03077.PDF (accessed 5 May 2020).

The Prosecutor v Ljube Boškoski and Johan Tarčulovski International Criminal Tribunal of the Former Yugoslavia, Trial Chamber II (IT-04-82-T) (10 July 2008).

The Prosecutor v Ramush Haradinaj, Idriz Balaj and Lahi Brahimaj International Criminal Tribunal of the Former Yugoslavia, Trial Chamber (IT-04-84-T) (3 April 2008).

T.M. Orugbo & Anor v Bulara Una & Ors (2002) LPELR-2778 (SC).

Umudge & Anor v Shell-BP Petroleum Development Company of Nigeria Limited (1975) 9-11 SC 155.
Yaki & Anor v Bagudu & Ors LPELR-25721 (SC) (2015).
Yampa & Ors v Babareke & Anor LPELR-41212 (CA) (2016).

Constitutions, national legislation, strategies and frameworks

Chad: Chad Penal Code (2017).
Child Rights Act (2003).
Constitution of the Arab Republic of Egypt (2014).
Constitution of the Federal Democratic Republic of Ethiopia (1994).
Constitution of the Federal Republic of Nigeria (1999).
Discrimination against Persons with Disabilities (Prohibition) Act (2018).
Federal Ministry of Humanitarian Affairs, Disaster Management and Social Development *National Policy on Internally Displaced Persons* (2021).
Federal Republic of Nigeria *National Policy on Internally Displaced Persons in Nigeria* (*Draft*, 2012).
Fundamental Rights (Enforcement Procedure) Rules (2009).
Geneva Conventions Act (1960).
Interpretation Act (1990).
Paris Agreement (2015).
Prevention, Protection and Assistance to Internally Displaced Persons and Affected Communities Act (2012).
Republic of Kenya National climate change action plan 2013–2017.
Rwanda: Law No 68/2018 of 30 August 2018: Law determining offences and penalties in general (2018).
National Commission for Refugees (Establishment, Etc) Act (2004).
National Emergency Management Agency (Establishment, Etc) Act (1999).
National Environmental Standards and Regulations Enforcement Act 2007.
Nigerian Minerals and Mining Act (2007).
National Plan for Comprehensive Care for People Displaced by Violence (2005).
Niger Law Relating to the Protection and Assistance of Internally Displaced Persons (2018).
Uganda: The National Policy for Internally Displaced Persons (2004).
Violence against Persons (Prohibition) Act (2015).
Zambia: Guidelines for the compensation and resettlement of internally displaced persons (2013).
Zimbabwe Human Rights Commission Action Plan on Durable Solutions on Forced Displacements in Africa (2019) (*draft*) (on file with author).

Reports, workshops and commentaries

Abebe, M Allehone 'The Kampala Convention and environmentally induced displacement in Africa' IOM Intersessional Workshop on Climate Change, Environmental Degradation and Migration, Geneva, Switzerland (29–30 March 2011).

Adekola, O Paul, Azuh, Dominic, Olawole-Isaac, Adebanke and Amoo, Emmanuel 'Health implication of development-induced internal displacements in Ogun state, Southwestern Nigeria' Proceedings of SOCIOINT 2017 – 4th International Conference on Education, Social Sciences and Humanities, Dubai, United Arab Emirates (10–12 July 2017).

Amnesty International *At the mercy of the government: violation of the right to an effective remedy in Badia East, Lagos state, Nigeria* (AFR 44/017/2014).

Amnesty International *Harvest of death: three years of bloody clashes between farmers and herders in Nigeria* (AFR/9503/2018).

Amnesty International *"Just move them": forced evictions in Port Harcourt, Nigeria* (2010).

Azam, Jean-Paul 'Betting on displacement: oil, violence, and the switch to civilian rule in Nigeria' Toulouse School of Economics Working Paper Series 09-034 (10 May 2009).

Cantor, J David and Apollo, O Jacob 'Internal displacement, internal migration and refugee flows: connecting the dots' (IDRP Research Briefing Paper, August 2020).

Casola, Camillo 'Multinational joint task force: security cooperation in the Lake Chad Basin' *Italian Institute for International Political Studies (Commentary)* (19 March 2020).

Center for Environmental Education and Development, Environmental Rights Action, GRAIN and Global Justice Now 'Dominion farms' land grab in Nigeria: farmers in Taraba state refuse to give up their lands for massive rice plantation project backed by the G8' (January 2015).

Centre on Housing Rights and Eviction and Social and Economic Rights Action Center *The myth of the Abuja master plan: Nigeria* (Mission Report, May 2008).

Decision 1/CP.16: The Cancun Agreements: Outcome of the work of the Ad Hoc Working Group on Long-term Cooperative Action under the Convention, adopted at the 16th Session of the United Nations Framework Convention on Climate Change Conference of the Parties, Cancun, Mexico (29 November – 10 December 2010).

'Declaration and action plan of the third AUC-NANHRI policy forum on the state of African National Human Rights Institutions held under the theme, "National Human Rights Institutions" contribution to durable solutions on forced displacements in Africa' (5–6 September 2019) (On file with author).

'Facing the challenge of the Islamic State in West Africa Province' International Crisis Group (Africa Report No 273, 16 May 2019).

Ferris, Elizabeth, Mooney, Erin and Stark, Chareen 'From responsibility to response: assessing national approaches to internal displacement' (2011) The Brookings Institution – London School of Economics Project on Internal Displacement.

Huma, Haider 'Climate change in Nigeria: impacts and responses' Knowledge, Evidence and Learning for Development (K4D) Helpdesk Report (10 October 2019).

Human Rights Watch *The price of oil: corporate responsibility and human rights violations in Nigeria's oil producing communities* (Human Rights Watch, 1999).

Internal Displacement Monitoring Centre and Norwegian Refugee Council 'Nigeria: multiple displacement crisis overshadowed by Boko Haram' (2014).

International Committee of the Red Cross Facts and figures: Nigeria in perspective: meeting evolving humanitarian needs (2017).

International Crisis Group *Herders against farmers: Nigeria's expanding deadly conflict* (Africa Report No 252, 19 September 2017).

International Law Commission *Draft articles on the protection of persons in the event of disaster* (2016).

Kaduna State Government *White Paper on the Report of the Committee to investigate causes of riots and disturbances in Kaduna State 6–12* March 1987.

Kaduna State of Nigeria *Report of Zangon Kataf (Market) riots judicial commission of inquiry* (June 1992).

Kaduna State of Nigeria *White paper on the report of Judicial Commission of Inquiry into Kaduna State religious disturbances of February 2000* (2001).

Kälin, Walter 'Guiding Principles on Internal Displacement: annotations' Studies in Transnational Legal Policy No 38, The American Society of International Law (2008).

Kekilli, Emrah, Omar, Khayri and Abdoulaye, B Ibrahim 'Anatomy of a terrorist organization: Boko Haram' (Foundation for Political, Economic and Social Research (SETA), 2018).

Krause, Jana 'A deadly cycle: ethno-religious conflict in Jos, Plateau state, Nigeria' (Geneva Declaration Secretariat Working Paper, June 2011).

Maurya, PR 'Farmer participation in irrigation development and management' Proceedings of a National Workshop held at the Institute for Agricultural Research, Samaru, Zaria, Nigeria (7–8 May 1990).

Minority Rights Group International *State of the World's minorities 2006 – Nigeria* (22 December 2005).

Moro, Leben 'Oil development induced displacement in the Sudan' Sir William Luce Fellowship Paper No 10, University of Durham, United Kingdom (2009).

Nigerian Senate *Interim report of the Senate Ad Hoc Committee on Southern Kaduna crisis and other parts of the country* (2017).

Report on Preliminary Examination Activities 2012 (November 2012).

Spaces for Change *Demolishing foundations of peace* (2012).

Terminski, Bogumil 'Oil-induced displacement and resettlement: social problem and human rights issue' Research Paper, School for International Studies, Simon Fraser University, Vancouver (2012).

United Nations Commission on Human Rights, Addendum 'Guiding Principles on Internal Displacement' Report of the Representative of the Secretary-General, Mr Francis M Deng, submitted pursuant to Commission on Human Rights resolution 1997/39, UN Doc. E/CN.4/1998/53/Add.2 (11 February 1998).

UN Commission on Human Rights, *Analytical Report of the Secretary-General on Internally Displaced Persons*, UN Doc E/CN.4/1992/23 (1992).

UN Commission on Human Rights, *Comprehensive Study on the Human Rights issues related to internally displaced persons*, prepared by Mr. Francis M. Deng, Representative of the Secretary-General, UN Doc E/CN.4/1993/35 (21 January 1993).

UN Commission on Human Rights 'Internally displaced persons: compilation and analysis of legal norms' Report of the Representative of the Secretary-General, Mr Francis M Deng submitted pursuant to the UN Commission on Human Rights resolution 1995/57, UN Doc. E/CN.4/1996/52/Add.2 (5 December 1995).

UN Human Rights Council, *Report of the Special Rapporteur on the right to privacy – right to privacy*, UN Doc A/HRC/40/63 (16 October 2019).

Vigil, Sara 'Green grabbing-induced displacement' (Istituto per gli Studi di Politica Internazionale (ISPI) Commentary, 23 March 2018).

World Bank *Groundswell: preparing for internal climate migration* (2018).

Media and other sources

'11 states yet to domesticate Child Rights Act – Minister' *Premium Times (Nigeria)* (13 October 2020).

African Union 'List of Countries which have signed, ratified/acceded to the African Charter on Human and Peoples' Rights' (2017).

African Union 'List of Countries which have signed, ratified/acceded to the African Union Convention for the Protection and Assistance of Internally Displaced Persons in Africa (Kampala Convention)' (2019).

Ahemba, Tume 'Nigeria evicted 800,000 Abuja residents: report' *Reuters* 15 May 2008.

Al-Hussaini, Bassim 'ISWAP, terror group in Nigeria, rebrands, reversing tradition' *Premium Times* 27 February 2020.

Anyanwu, Samuel 'Ministry of Humanitarian Affairs, FCT Ministry set up Joint Committee on IDPs welfare' *Federal Ministry of Information and Culture (Press Releases)* 10 March 2020 https://fmic.gov.ng/ministry-of-humanitarian-affairs-fct-ministry-setup-joint-committee-on-idps-welfare/ (accessed 6 May 2020).

'Armed gang kills at least 30 in northwest Nigeria, police say' *Reuters* 15 February 2020.

Arsenault, Chris 'Nigerian farmers face eviction by foreign mega-plantation – TRFN' *Reuters* 28 January 2015.

'At least 50 killed in northern Nigeria "bandit" attacks' *Al Jazeera* 2 March 2020.

Bellal, Annyssa 'ICRC commentary of Common Article 3: some questions relating to organized armed groups and the applicability of IHL' *EJIL: Talk!* 5 October 2017.

'Boko haram conflict causing misery to millions 10 years on' *Norwegian Refugee Council* 23 July 2019.

'Boko Haram islamists still control parts of northeastern Nigeria' *DW* 19 May 2018.

'Brutal violence in northern Nigeria forces thousands into Niger' *UN Refugee Agency* 27 September 2019.

'Chadian troops "kill 1,000 Boko Haram fighters" in Lake Chad' *Al Jazeera* 9 April 2020.

Counter Extremism Project *Boko Haram* (2002).

Eizenga, Daniel 'Chad's escalating fight against Boko Haram' *Africa Center for Strategic Studies (Spotlight)* 20 April 2020.

Federal Government of Nigeria *First regional conference on internal displacement in West Africa* (26-28 April 2006) https://www.brookings.edu/wp-content/upl oads/2012/04/ECOWAS_rpt_FINAL.pdf (accessed 2 March 2021).

'Fighting Boko Haram in Chad: beyond military measures' *International Crisis Group* (Africa Report No 246, 8 March 2017).

Hartley, Will 'Re-emergence of Ansaru in northern Nigeria raises threat of targeted violence against western nationals and companies' *Jane's Terrorism & Insurgency Monitor* 23 January 2020.

Haruna, Abdulkareem 'Special report: increasing Boko Haram attacks on highways threaten to cut Borno state from Nigeria' *Premium Times* 23 January 2020.

'How is the term "armed conflict" defined in international humanitarian law?' International Committee of the Red Cross (ICRC) Opinion Paper (March 2008) 3 https://www.icrc.org/en/doc/assets/files/other/opinion-paper-armed-conflict .pdf (accessed 5 May 2020).

International Committee of the Red Cross 'Facts & Figures: ICRC in Nigeria' (January–June 2019).

'Lawlessness double displaced from NW Nigeria to 40,000 – UNHCR' *Euronews* 27 September 2019.

Intergovernmental Panel on Climate Change *Global warming of 1.5°C* (Intergovernmental Panel on Climate Change, 2019).

Iroanusi, QueenEsther 'Senate laments lack of cooperation between NEMA, SEMA, others' *Premium Times* 10 November 2020.

'Key migration terms' https://www.iom.int/key-migration-terms (accessed 25 August 2021).

Kulungu, Mustapha 'Does Boko Haram pose a threat to the US?' (2019) 11(2) *Counter Terrorist Trends and Analyses* https://www.jstor.org/stable/pdf/26627975.pdf?refr eqid=excelsior%3Aaf25f74202b62f361b9d8bb1c77eb83f (accessed 5 May 2020).

'Motorcycle gang on the rampage in Nigeria' *Defence Web* 17 February 2020.

National Human Rights Commission 'Refugees, internally displaced persons, migrants and asylum seekers' https://www.nigeriarights.gov.ng/focus-areas/ refugees-internally-displaced-persons-migrants-and-asylum-seekers.html (accessed 2 March 2021).

'Niger army repels Boko Haram attack, 50 extremists killed – govt' *Africa News* 17 March 2020 https://www.youtube.com/watch?v=TbcpEh_s1xA (accessed 5 May 2020).

'Nigeria's Boko Haram "seize" Bama town in Borno' *BBC (News)* 2 September 2014.

'Nigeria – Child marriage around the world' *Girls Not Brides* https://www.girlsnot brides.org/child-marriage/nigeria/ (accessed 6 May 2020).

'Nigeria president condemns latest killings in northwestern Sokoto state' *Reuters* 20 July 2019.

'Nigeria says it has ousted Boko Haram from town of Bama' *BBC (News)* 17 March 2015.

Nnodim, Okechukwu 'NEMA prepares against flooding' *Punch* 30 April 2019.

Nossiter, Adam 'New threat in Nigeria as militants split off' *The New York Times* 23 April 2013.

Nugent, John 'Boko Haram's leadership crisis' *Forbes* 20 September 2013.

122   Bibliography

McGrath, Matt 'Climate change: '"Hothouse Earth"' risks even if CO2 emissions slashed' *BBC News* 6 August 2018.

Munshi, Neil 'Overwhelmed by bandits, Nigeria state offer amnesty' *Financial Times* 13 October 2019.

Oladipo, Emmanuel 'Towards enhancing the adaptive capacity in Nigeria: a review of the country's state of preparedness for climate change adaptation' Henrich Böll Foundation Nigeria (September 2010) https://ng.boell.org/sites/default/files/uplo ads/2013/10/nigeria_prof_oladipo_final_cga_study.pdf (accessed 6 May 2020).

Omotola, J Shola 'Explaining electoral violence in Africa's "new" democracies' *Accord* AJCR 2010/3 https://www.accord.org.za/ajcr-issues/explaining-electoral-violen ce-in-africas-new-democracies/ (accessed 6 May 2020).

'Over 30,000 homeless after police use demolition by fire and bulldozer working in dead of night destroy Otodo Gbame community despite subsisting injunction' *Justice & Empowerment Initiative – Nigeria* (Press Release, 10 November 2016) https://static1.squarespace.com/static/535d0435e4b0586b1fc64b54/t/582412f56 a49630e4fdb3b06/1478759158239/Otodo+Gbame+Press+Release+%28Nov +10+2016%29.pdf (accessed 6 May 2020).

Raphelson, Samantha 'Islamic state group in Nigeria reportedly executes Christian hostages' *NPR* 27 December 2019.

'Resistance continues to ending child marriage in northern Nigeria' *VOA* 22 March 2018 https://www.youtube.com/watch?v=VI_U3tlkWd8 (accessed 6 May 2020).

'Responding to the needs of people affected by armed conflict in Yobe state, Nigeria' International Committee of the Red Cross (Article) 29 July 2019.

Sampson, Akanimo 'Don't sell forests, groups urge Nigerian govts' *Scoop (World)* 27 August 2010 https://www.scoop.co.nz/stories/WO1008/S00467/dont-sell-fore sts-groups-urge-nigerian-govts.htm (accessed 6 May 2020).

Sampson, T Isaac 'Religious violence in Nigeria' *Accord* AJCR 2012/1 https://www .accord.org.za/ajcr-issues/religious-violence-in-nigeria/ (accessed 6 May 2020).

Sinclair, Stephanie 'Child, bride, mother: Nigeria' *New York Times* 27 January 2017.

Sunday, Orji 'It rains, it pours, it floods: Nigeria's growing seasonal problem' *African Arguments* 15 November 2018.

'Supplement' *Oxford Learner's Dictionaries* https://www.oxfordlearnersdictionar ies.com/definition/english/supplement_1?q=supplement (6 May 2020).

'The North East Development Commission (NEDC)' *Medium* 8 May 2019.

Tukur, Sani 'Buhari inaugurates board of North East Development Commission' *Premium Times* 8 May 2019.

'Violence in Niger Delta expands into gang war' *CNN* 8 August 2007.

With gangs aplenty, Lagos inner streets know little joy' *The Guardian (Nigeria)* 13 November 2018.

Yagboyaju, A Dhikru and Akinola, O Adeoye 'Nigerian state and the crisis of governance: a critical exposition' (2019) *SAGE Open* https://doi.org/10.1177 /2158244019865810 (accessed 6 May 2020).

Zenn, Jacob 'Islamic state in West Africa province's factional disputes and the battle with Boko Haram' (2020) 18(6) *Terrorism Monitor* 6 https://jamestown.org/pro gram/islamic-state-in-west-africa-provinces-factional-disputes-and-the-battle -with-boko-haram/ (accessed 5 May 2020).

Index

Note: Page numbers with "n" indicates the end notes in the text.

For Product Safety Concerns and Information please contact our EU
representative GPSR@taylorandfrancis.com
Taylor & Francis Verlag GmbH, Kaufingerstraße 24, 80331 München, Germany